The Hollywood Food Chain

The Hollywood Food Chain

A Comically Real Look at Hollywood through the Eyes of Production Assistants

Tiffany Carboni

Writer's Showcase
presented by *Writer's Digest*
San Jose New York Lincoln Shanghai

The Hollywood Food Chain
A Comically Real Look at Hollywood through
the Eyes of Production Assistants

Writer's Showcase
presented by *Writer's Digest*
an imprint of iUniverse.com, Inc.

For information address:
iUniverse.com, Inc.
620 North 48th Street, Suite 201
Lincoln, NE 68504-3467
www.iuniverse.com

ISBN: 0-595-13001-1

Printed in the United States of America

Contents

The Hollywood Food Chain

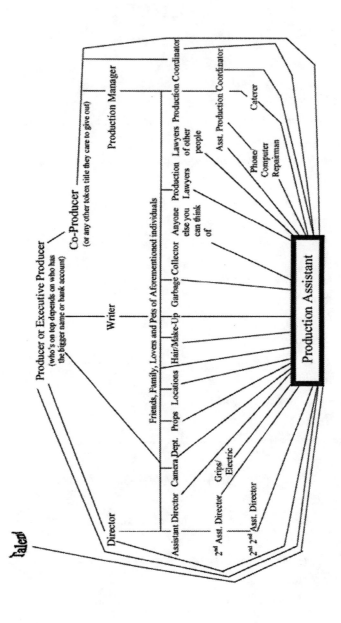

Acknowledgements

I'd like to thank all my friends and fellow Production Assistants who humored me with their many stories. I'd like to especially bow down to those who thought they didn't have anything worth telling and ended up talking for hours of their Hollywood moments.

Thanks to my parents, Gayle and Vic, who supported and encouraged me to embark on the foreign road of freelance work without too many lectures on the importance of job stability and benefits. And to Sean, who always encourages me to be the best I can be.

Last, but never least, I am grateful to all those Hollywoodites who constantly give us all amusing stories worth telling.

—Tiffany Carboni

Introduction

Amidst the fierce jungles of filmmaking lies a hierarchy of jobs needing to be filled in order for any movie or television show to be successfully completed. We all know the wise and mighty leaders who are glorified in the tireless Hollywood fashion. You know, the directors, producers, and of course the *stars*.

But despite popular belief, it takes many more people than that to make the shows we watch look effortless. Hail to the little people of tinsel town who put in the grueling hours to make sure life runs with relative ease for the bigwigs. In the pages to come, we salute those people who fall into the lowest rungs of the Hollywood food chain (and pay scale)—the production assistants.

It's difficult to define the duties of a PA because they are ever changing day to day, job to job. Production assistants are given some of the most obscure, bizarre and completely absurd jobs in either an office or on a set.

This isn't a technical "how-to" to production assisting. Many of these stories are first hand experiences. Others came from friends and acquaintances at countless "below the line" parties where the purpose was to get drunk, eat Cheetos, and gossip about job horror stories. In any case, names have been changed to protect the innocent (and not so innocent who could hurt us).

CHAPTER ONE

The Seedling of a Great Idea

When I was in high school, I had dreams of moving to Hollywood where those important movie people on high would HAVE to discover me. I was destined to become a movie star. Then I tried out for a school play and got the glamorous part of a backstage techie.

Ouch! That one really hurt my ego. Couldn't the drama teacher see that I was going to be the next Meryl Streep?

I walked through the school's halls like a zombie with my mouth frozen open in shock for hours. Still determined to be a part of the show, I settled for the duties behind the scenes. During the weeks and weeks of rehearsals, I came to realize that I really loved being a stealth part of the theatre—the part that no one in the audience really, well…cared about.

The opening night whipped the cast and crew into an absolute frenzy. I kept my cool and became the most relied upon person in the wings because I was so spectacular at my backstage job. Actually I was the only one back there who wasn't stoned.

After each performance, the actors were greeted with flowers and praise from friends and relatives while I would come out wearing my required hidden-behind-the-curtains black outfit from head to toe. I got a few strange looks from the crowd as if to ask, "Where's the funeral?" Other than that no one paid me much attention. They were too busy glorifying those especially talented people in costumes. Zzzzzz!

Instead of feeling bitter and wanting to push the arrogantly popular lead actress down the stairs, I walked away from the theatre full of confidence and satisfaction.

After a few more years of allowing high school theatre to seep through and take over my brain like a bad horror flick, I went to college. To my amazement they had this extraordinary major called Film Studies. Could this really be? They would give me a Bachelor of Arts degree from a good university and all I had to do was watch movies until my butt hurt?

One day during the last quarter of my senior year, I stopped dead in my tracks to evaluate my life. Where was I headed with this fancy schmancy film degree? I knew I wanted to write, produce, direct, edit, drink, and sleep film. But, without a huge bankroll and no real experience for anything besides being a college party animal, how was a major movie studio going to pay me to write and direct the next *Jaws*?

And then it happened, right there at the food court in the university's student center. I decided to let Hollywood use, abuse and take advantage of me.

Trumpets, please!

I would become an overworked, underpaid production assistant!

CHAPTER TWO

Planes, Trains, But Mostly Automobiles

Production assistant. Doesn't that sound like a classy title? It evokes visions of Hollywood glamour mixed with a hint of reckless career opportunities. Forget your nine to five office crap, this is the kind of work most parents fear for their children—freelance work!

To outsiders, it's a job title that inspires thoughts of extravagant hob-nobbing with an impressive list of celebrities worth bragging about. It arouses images of merciless schmoozing with great directors and interesting foreign producers. Ah, the alluring life of a PA.

Perhaps in good time these romantic notions will happen for a PA, but in general, this is a job that encompasses so much more than all that silly *stuff*. The focus is more on hard-core important matters like picking up lunches and delivering scripts and…and…and driving. And I don't mean driving; I mean drrrriiiiiiiivvvvvvvvving for hours and hours on the highways and byways of greater Los Angeles and beyond.

Get Yer All-Risk Insurance

I have only driven a few cars in my lifetime—mainly those that have belonged to my family and perhaps the occasional bumper car at Disneyland. People don't generally trust me with their automobiles. I tend to get carried away when a really good tune comes over the radio and I just dance uncontrollably in my seat. I am currently in a twelve-step program for Dancers and Drivers Anonymous.

Through my years of PA-dom, driving different kinds of vehicles allowed me to meet the most interesting types of people. While working on a near nothing budget film, I had to go to a nearby Rent-a-Crap dealer to rent a seventeen foot cube truck—the vehicle of choice for all those sultry Beverly Hills trend setters. I dealt with a gentleman who was a couple of ice cubes short of a cool drink. His name was Rocky and by his appearance I was guessing he was a motorcycle aficionado who could distinguish a fine can of 1030 from 1040 motor oil solely by smell.

By the carcinogenic cloud lingering in the shop, I figured he hadn't heard about the effects that chain smoking had on furniture. It looked like he had fallen asleep a few too many times on his easy chair while watching his thirteen inch black and white television with rabbit ears.

This might be a shocker for some, but sometimes a PA's best weapon is other people's ignorance. Hey, it's a tough world out there for PAs. You've got to take any advantage you can grab.

As you know, rules were made for everyone **except** those who are too busy making important entertainment for the rest of the world. You could say the world of media and all its self-made hype is as important as, if not *more* so than, the world of politics and its government officials who create world peace treaty policies. Think about it, everyone always needs to be entertained—even when there are wars going on. At least that's what Hollywood would like everyone to believe.

In the window of this car rental facility/gas station, a sign clearly threatened that if you weren't twenty-five years old, you weren't renting a vehicle here. That petty little detail left me a measly three years, nine months, and sixteen days shy of this lucky car renting age. Although Sean, the producer, was well over twenty-five years of age, he pushed my license in front of Rocky rather than offering his own.

Why? Did Sean think he was too good to play by the rules? Did he want to keep his identity hidden from the public? No, his license had expired two months ago and he never bothered to renew it. I could have rung his neck. This was the producer, the boss, the man *in charge* of the entire film. And he was one traffic violation away from some major headaches. What a great team we made.

The Rockster looked at my identification and asked how old I was.

"Twenty-five, of course," I replied.

He desperately tried to figure out if I was telling the truth based on my printed birth date. After finally pulling out a calculator, he realized I was a mere twenty-one years of age. He gave me the eye—he only had one to offer.

I laughed nervously and asked, "Is it my fault that I am age challenged. What are years anyway besides a system our corrupt government has put upon us to create discrimination?"

I shut my eyes and wondered which of the two men were going to yell at me first, Rocky who was scrunching up his forehead or Sean who was starting to froth at the mouth.

Rocky replied in his gruff monotone, "You're right, kid. %$!@ the government and their %$!@-ing rules. Sign here."

I felt like an idiot for having judged his intelligence so harshly.

Then we got to the big challenge of the day. To buy insurance or not to buy insurance—that was the question? Rocky was offering a special for that day only—ALL-RISK INSURANCE FOR FIVE DOLLARS.

"All-risk, really?" I asked. "So what if we hit and kill a group of elderly people while driving the truck? Would five dollars really cover the mess?"

The poor gentleman took a long drag from his cigarette and held it so long I had my fingers ready to dial 9-1-1. He finally exhaled right in my face and scratched his head. He had obviously never been asked such a technical question about his policy.

After an uncomfortably drawn out pause, he replied, "Uh, I guess so." And off we went to the parking lot in search of the perfect truck.

All three of us walked up and down the rows of rental trucks looking for the best one to hold all of our camera equipment. We had only one demand for whichever truck we walked away with—it had to be secure because it was going to be left on the street over night.

As we strolled across the vast lot…okay, okay…there were two trucks to choose from in the corner of this shabby gas station's lot.

We had to choose between the truck with no bumper, a crack in the windshield on the driver's side, a hole the size of a watermelon in the cab's floor, and no door handles—**or** the one that blew thick black exhaust after we tried to turn the engine over a mere sixteen times. Sean and I stood there for at least a half hour debating over which was the **least** worst.

Rocky determined we should take the bumper-less truck after playing Eenie, Meenie, Minie, Mo. Sean stepped in the cab and closed the door. The slam made the window slide open on its own. Rocky slipped quietly back inside his office.

I got into Sean's little sports car. After all, I had no intention of driving anything that was bigger than my apartment. Then it hit both of us like a Mack truck in the gut—I couldn't drive Sean's car. It was a stick shift! Oh the horror. Why had I resisted my dad's suggestions to learn?

Now wasn't the time to dwell on regrets. I had a lot of learning to do in the next thirty seconds. But Sean wasn't about to have me learn on his prized automobile.

Instead, I got a crash course in driving a gigantic automatic cube truck that was just shy of being as large as the Titanic. Actually I got the hang of it pretty quickly after nearly taking out a couple of mailboxes and scaring a few people off the sidewalk. I figured, hey, this is Los Angeles. They've seen worse drivers, and more impressively, I wasn't even waving a gun.

When I pulled up to the set with the monster mobile, I got a standing ovation from the other production assistants. I was named honorary transpo captain for the day. You see, the film was so low budget that they actually had no transportation department at all. If there had been such a necessary department, there would have been no reason for me to endanger the entire population of Los Angeles. A professional teamster could have done it for triple my salary.

Cruisin' in the Rover

Because I was so good at this driving thing, my next conquest was a $70,000 top of the line Range Rover. It was our picture vehicle borrowed from a car salesman who was under the impression we were considering purchasing the vehicle. Personally, I can't believe anyone could think our crew should have been entrusted with anything more valuable than a folding chair. Especially Sean who had by then lost his driver's license completely.

Over the film's two month shoot, the beautiful sport utility vehicle was to be used in a mere three scenes. While the car wasn't needed for a shot in the film, the production team had me use the grossly high-priced, luxury SUV to run essential errands like picking up herbal medicines, frappamochas, and fruit smoothies.

I think there was something funky in the herbal medicine that made them think it was okay to allow a twenty-one-year-old, who could not help herself from dancing while driving, to drive a car that was worth more than her college education. However, there was no other choice because I didn't have my own car at the time and no one was offering up theirs.

I was having the time of my life in that Rover. The stereo system was amazing. I couldn't believe the exhilaration of riding higher than all the other puny cars around me. I felt like a go-go dancer on a stage bee-bopping to my favorite tunes. It was great…while I was parked in the driveway.

The idea of actually driving that thing on the battlefield of Ventura Boulevard inspired stomach cramping. I was so afraid of crashing the car and messing up the film's continuity, not to mention the non-existent budget. Each time I started the motor, I crossed my fingers and said a little prayer to the film gods atop the Hollywood Hills that I would bring it back unharmed. I was so edgy that I honked the horn whenever I came within fifteen feet of another car. My nerves were so overloaded that I could not turn the music on for fear I would dance.

I tried to explain to Sean that I shouldn't drive because of all the what-ifs. He laughed at my insecurities and pointed out that it was either the Rover or his stick shift. So, the automatic Range Rover carried me all over town for weeks. I was going through such serious dance withdrawals that I was shaking when I returned to the production office. But it was all for the good of the film, I kept telling myself. But the stress and anguish were taking its toll on me. I would wake up in the middle of the night drenched in sweat imagining I had lost my groove.

After weeks of putting myself through this nightmare, it ended up that one of the actresses plowed the exotic vehicle into the garage wall in the middle of a take. She managed to smash both taillights and severely dent the bumper. Let us all take a moment to bow our heads for the poor Range Rover.

Lovely Day for a Police Pursuit

Before that actress saved me from the torment of having to drive the spanking new Rover with no license plates, I was pulled over by a cop. He claimed it was some nonsense about me not making a complete stop…blah, blah, blah.

We started to talk it up as I fished around for my driver's license. I mentioned I was working on a film. He got excited and told me his heartbreaking story of how he wanted to be an actor so badly but he got booed off his high school stage. We laughed and talked some more until he inevitably asked again for my driver's license and registration.

I went to the glove compartment to retrieve the registration. The cop and I saw it was completely empty…except for a gun that fell to the floor. Both of our mouths dropped open wider than the glove compartment.

The officer drew his gun on me and commanded me to get out of the car with my hands up. I tried to explain that the gun was a fake used in a scene earlier that morning. I cursed the ground my crew walked on. This was probably a malicious setup spawned by Sean's horrible sense of humor.

The officer told me to slowly get my driver's license from my purse. Wouldn't you know it, I had left my purse at the production office.

After what seemed like forever (and about sixteen thousand gallons of sweat and tears on my part), this compassionate cop listened to my incredulous story. He checked out the gun and immediately saw it was a fake. He then called the station to verify I had a license.

I wrapped myself around his ankle sobbing and begging him not to arrest me. He had a good belly laugh that lasted like five minutes while I waved at the gawking passersby. When he finally stopped laughing, he told me he was letting me go under one condition.

Yes, what? I'd do anything.

He said, "You're free if I can use your story."

For the police report? Damn it, did this mean I was going to have a record? Wait a minute, was I going to be on an episode of "COPS?" I told him to shoot me right then and there if this whole fiasco had been videotaped for public display.

"No," he assured me. "I want the rights to your story. I'm a cop by day, screenwriter by night." He gave me his card and promised we would do lunch someday. You gotta love Hollywood.

I Left My Heart in...Bakersfield?

Pete was working on his very first film. It was a short. The ad in the paper promised "lots of fun with great people, decent hours and money."

The ad should have read: "Looking for strong-willed PA with an iron gut for cruel people. Don't expect to become rich. Consider food as payment. And the hours—ha, ha, we own you!"

Pete was so eager to get attached to any sort of film production. He was willing to overlook the fact that the entire crew, especially Trudy the producer, was a group of dysfunctional delinquents.

On his first day, he was given the responsibility of driving the film's equipment (camera package, lights, sound, props, and costumes) to the Bakersfield location from Los Angeles. He felt honored to be trusted with so much responsibility. Though, it was quickly apparent that no one else wanted the job and it had been passed on down the food chain.

The hardworking grips and electricians helped *watch* Pete load up the truck. Occasionally one of them would lend a finger to *point out* that he should put a heavy case on the other side of the truck to distribute the weight. Then these guys would redistribute *their* weight by stuffing an easily accessible donut into their mouths before washing it down with a cold brewskie.

One thing you can count on from a grip or electrician is that no matter how tough the job is (to watch) they **always** carry cold beers. Even if they can't find their tool belts, they can always find their cooler.

Pete, being the fresh college graduate, knew that accepting this PA job meant he was restricted from complaining about it. He figured there was plenty of time to do that later when he was a high-rolling Hollywood player with his very own staff of six thousand.

Despite the cube truck's broken air conditioner, its AM radio, a terribly rough engine and a gas tank that needed nourishment every seven miles, Pete decided to embrace the challenge and head out into the rebellious freedom of the open road.

The hellion rebellion in him keeled over in boredom waiting in a huge line of smelly, diesel emitting big rigs at a weigh station somewhere near nowhere on Interstate 5.

After a quick inspection, the truck weighers determined Pete's cube truck was way over its legal weight limit. Uh, oh. Pete was not prepared for this crisis. He started to pound his head.

Wait a minute, this wasn't a problem, he was working on a *movie*. They had to bend the rules for him. He quickly put a smile on his face and explained everything to the kind highway patrol officer who was fingering his gun like a mentally imbalanced cowboy.

The officer carefully looked Pete over and said, "Son, you're going to have to pull the hell over." Pete remained calm despite the sweat stinging his eyes. He'd have this straightened out in no time.

Unfortunately, those highway patrol officers treated him as pleasantly as if he had just committed armed robbery. Pete kept his cool and reiterated that he was working on a film and that he'd love it if they could cut him a break. The officers did not find that funny. In fact, by order of the California Highway Patrol Ordinance 1258.42.62 1/2 3/4"A, these men were not allowed to find anything funny. All Pete wanted was for them to at least take off their Erik Estrada sunglasses. But they wouldn't even give him the satisfaction of doing that.

So Pete sat there on the side of the highway inside the beat up, smelly truck somewhere in the San Joaquin Valley in the middle of a sweltering August. He kept going over the promises that Trudy had made that morning when she said he only had to work a partial day (ten hours instead of sixteen) for a whole thirty dollars. At the rate he was going, he would be lucky to get off after an eighteen hour day. At that moment, he was very proud of where his college degree had taken him.

Pete tried to call the hotel in Bakersfield where the crew was staying that evening. Unfortunately, the phone number had mysteriously disappeared along with his sense of humor. He finally got a hold of the hotel only to discover that no one had arrived yet.

To complicate matters, there was no one left at the production office in Los Angeles. He was running out of change and patience. He thought about making a break from the weigh station, but the idea of spending the night in jail wasn't too appealing. Although, jail was probably air-conditioned and he could use a meal.

The sun was starting to set as he called the hotel again. This time he got a hold of Tracy. It turned out that she had been there the entire time pampering herself with a mud bath and didn't want to be disturbed. When he was finally able to make contact with her at the poolside phone, she was horrorstruck at the news that her expensive equipment was laying around "unprotected on the side of the road somewhere."

Pete assured her, "We're all fine here. Thanks for asking."

In a voice of sheer Hollywood producer annoyance, as though Pete was responsible for this fiasco, she told him, "God, this is such an inconvenience to me. Now sit there. Don't move until someone comes to get the equipment."

Yeah, thanks for the tip lady, he thought. There Pete sat for hours somewhere between Limbo and Hell and watched the sun disappear over the mountain peaks. To keep his brain stimulated, he broke down his $30 day rate into an hourly wage—he was thankful there were no sharp objects in view.

Sometime before midnight, and well after the CHP officers went home, a couple of grips in a pickup truck came to *watch* Pete unload the extra weight from the truck.

Counting Planes to Fall Asleep

Thanks to Felicia's spectacular reputation for being a hard worker and her outstanding connections, she landed herself a dream job as a PA on a mongo budget film with two mega stars and a world-renowned director. This film was going to be immense for her career.

This opportunity hadn't come easily for her. She had paid her dues on many low or no-paying films and now it was time to reap the glory. Oh baby, she could taste the success already!

On the set, Felicia was kicking some serious butt to get herself known. Right away the director took notice at how diligent she was. Subsequently, Harvey, the executive producer, found out what a phenomenal PA she was and took her aside. He had a very, **very** important job that he would entrust to only her.

He said, "Go to the Lexus dealership in Van Nuys..."

He was referring to a location that was being highly considered for their shoot later that month.

"Yeah, yeah?" she asked anxiously awaiting the exciting assignment. She knew it. He was going to make her a location manager. That was a great job; the money and prestige would be spectacular. She figured Harvey heard about her outstanding negotiation skills and wanted her to hammer out a great deal for the site. Her heart was galloping; her smile took over her entire face as he continued.

"...And count how many planes you can hear over an eight hour period," Harvey said as though he was a coach psyching up his team. However, his team did not think this was such a hot assignment.

Felicia, of course, did not protest. She closed her hanging mouth and thanked Harvey for thinking she was trustworthy enough to count planes.

At the car dealership, she sat in her car for about two and a half hours and seriously counted planes. There were a good sixty or so of them; from tiny buzzing commuter planes to loud, booming 747 jets. You see, there was a small airport behind the site and the executive producer was afraid that the planes could be a potential sound nightmare.

A deaf monkey could have told him the dealership was a horrible location. She was upset that her talents were being wasted on something so brainless. But she refused to let it get her down. Instead, she went with the flow—and went to get her car washed.

The next morning she handed Harvey a spreadsheet on which she fictitiously detailed the kinds of planes that flew over her head within the supposed eight hours. She "recorded" how often they flew overhead and rated them for sound disturbance. This took her about fifteen minutes to complete as she watched Oprah solve someone's life problem.

Harvey loved it. He loved her. He promised they'd do lunch soon. Felicia rolled her eyes and shook her head.

After the film was finished, Harvey offered Felicia a full-time job as a nanny to his three dogs at his Malibu mansion. She was appalled. After all the hours she had put in, after all the brain cells she had destroyed for that film, after all those pounds she had put on from stress bingeing—well, the daily glazed donuts were really delicious. However, as soon as he told her how much he was going to pay her, she jumped at the position immediately.

The job surprised her. Between dog grooming sessions and walks, Felicia was meeting and lunching with Harvey's friends who were some of Hollywood's biggest players. Thanks to her talents as a pooper-scooper she now has a screenplay in development with Harvey's best friend's production company.

Move 'em Out

Brad was working his PA magic on a film with a budget so small, you needed a microscope to find it. How tight was their money? It was so tight that Skip, the producer, couldn't afford to hire a transportation department despite the fact that this was a *Duke's of Hazard* type film.

Brad and the three other PAs were those lucky few in charge of returning all ten of the picture cars to the rental lot in Van Nuys.

After spending thirteen hours on the set, Brad and his PA cronies watched in jealousy as the rest of the crew headed home. The PAs had at least two hours of work left ahead of them (providing traffic was decent) by returning these clunkers.

They each hit the road in their respective vehicles only to discover the 101 freeway was jammed solid. That certainly didn't come as a shocker to any of them, but they weren't happy about it.

Brad could feel the road rage grab hold of him, but he remained calm—though he seriously contemplated abandoning the car on the freeway's fast lane during one of many dead stops. Onward the PAs traveled knowing they still had more vehicles to return.

On their second trip back to the car rental lot (an hour and seventeen minutes later), the traffic was even worse. All Brad wanted was to kick off his shoes and fall into his soft bed. Maybe he would accidentally forget to set his alarm clock.

His tired eyes were burning. He kept shaking himself awake. Wouldn't that be ironic, he thought, to die at the wheel of an ambulance?

An ambulance! He was driving the ambulance. Okay, so it wasn't the real thing…but look—the siren switch. He couldn't resist. He flicked the switch—and it worked! So did the lights. The cars in front of him pulled over immediately allowing him to pass. Instantly, he was cleared for takeoff. You better believe he took advantage of it before the cops came after him.

Suddenly, he saw a police car trailing him. Uh oh, he was in for it. He carefully looked through the rearview mirror to get a good look at the cop. It was Steve, his PA buddy. Cool, at least they were going to hell together.

CHAPTER THREE

Crazy Auteurs

Directors are some of the most intriguing behind-the-scenes individuals. They are considered the "authors" of the films whose artistic visions illuminate the screens. They take the words from the pages and throw them into life. They are almost godlike because they are the only ones who can boss the biggest stars around.

They can also be the biggest pains in human existence, or at least PA existence.

The Pool Looks Mighty Wet

FADE IN: The camera pans across a roomful of out of focus pandemonium. Slowly, the picture becomes clear and we see that we are in the director's house shooting a low budget film starring a couple of impressive actors.

A director using his own house as a location? Now, everyone press your hands against your face and scream Macaulay Culkin style, "Arrrghhh!"

It's just a bad idea, particularly if that thirty-six-year-old director is so anal retentive that he still has his mom iron his underwear.

It had been two and a half months of shooting. The anxiety had been increasing as a result of the cramped quarters. The working conditions inside the confines of the single story, one bedroom house were miserable. On this particular day, the tension was running even higher than normal because of a complicated pool scene.

It was a tiny backyard of which the pool took up like ninety-seven percent. This left a whopping three by seven-foot sliver of a walkway for the seventy-five person crew to take care of their business.

The grips were moving the lights, the electricians were flagging the lights, the camera department was setting up the camera and the hair and make-up people were taking care of the actors. Walkie-talkies squawked as frustrated crew members talked over one another.

Despite all the hard work that was going on, all the director seemed to see was the crew screwing around. He was so sick and tired of all these people being in his house for so long that he had become snippy at everyone. By that point, everyone knew far too much about the man—even down to what kind of medicine he used to cure his jock itch and where he kept his nose hair clippers.

Despite all the chaos, not everyone was determined to make this such a horrible ordeal. The jovial camera operator was joking around with the make-up lady like nothing in the world was wrong. The director didn't like this and stormed over to them.

As the director pushed his way through the crowd, he accidentally intercepted the camera assistant's expensive electronic clapper and Charles, the PA. Both Charles and the clapper flew into the pool. The whole crew stopped and gasped as they noticed the belt full of walkie-talkies attached to Charles' waist as he went sinking to the bottom. Some people covered their eyes in fright while others tried to find a pole. Through the panic, everyone was thinking the same thing—those radios were going to cost a fortune to replace.

Charles was a little more worried about the *shock* factor of electricity in water. After all, his medical insurance hadn't kicked in yet.

Charles managed to undo the belt with the radios and pulled his waterlogged body out of the pool. All the while, everyone just watched in horror—no one wanted to get their hair wet.

The director just looked at Charles and said, "Who do you think is going to pay for all those walkie talkies?"

The Human Bloodhound

A B-film director with more ego than brains asked me if I would take him to his mechanic's garage to pick up his car after we wrapped for the day. I agreed, but only because I couldn't come up with a plausible excuse fast enough. After a long day that started at 5 a.m., I led this oddly wanna-be-hip fifty-seven-year-old man to my car. His wild, hot pink pants, purple Converse shoes and long, wild silver hair suggested he might be a fun conversationalist. He appeared to be kind of arty with an eclectic view of life.

Boy, was I wrong.

With a blatant disregard for anything that was not his, he pushed himself into my precious dance floor, er, I mean my car. He looked me square in the eyes and said, "Do you know how to drive, or what? Chop, chop."

I bit my lip and refused to let it get to me. That was until he started violently shoving my passenger seat and complained how uncomfortable my car was. I didn't even allow it to bother me when he adjusted my rearview mirror to admire himself. But I nearly lost it when he wiped gobs of mud off his shoe onto my floor mat. But I remained focused on the duty at hand—getting him to his mechanic and out of my car.

I wondered aloud if this mechanic of his would still be open at that late hour. "He's on my payroll, so he's my employee, so he does what I say," spouted the patronizing linguist. So much for the small talk on this trip.

Before I started the car, I did what any good PA would do, I referred to my Thomas Guide (the bible of all map books) to figure out where I was going. He exploded into a tirade adamantly insisting he knew how to get there because he was a "human bloodhound." I said nothing although I wanted to laugh so badly at his foolish outburst. The man had a salivation problem. Every time he yelled, he started to spit and drool like a mad dog.

He wiped his mouth but wasn't sure what to do with the wet mess. He waited until he thought I wasn't watching and wiped it on the back of the headrest.

Then he demanded I tune the radio to his favorite classical station. He explained that my "X-Generation, artistically repressed, over sexed, drugged out raucous" was too hard on his "flawless, aesthetically trained ear."

I told him the radio was busted and turned it off. We drove along in an uncomfortable silence for about a half hour. He just sat there drooling.

We finally made our way into the San Fernando Valley. He started snapping directions at me. After driving past the same 7-Eleven and plastic surgeon's office for the sixth time, I knew I had to do something. In an effort to solve the problem without him feeling foolish, I kindly offered my Thomas Guide again. Bubbles started to creep out through his nose. He insisted that if he could direct a cast of two hundred in an epic (piece of crap) film, he could direct me to the garage. He put his hand to his forehead as though the answer was going to come to him by some sort of psychic power.

I sat and stared at him with droopy, tired eyes wishing I was capable of making him vanish into thin air. I had been working for sixteen hours already. I was getting tired and hungry. I wanted to go to sleep and this guy was more concerned about the new Starbucks on the corner.

I discreetly took the Thomas Guide out to search for the mechanic's street myself. He snarled and ripped the book out of my hands hurling it brutally into the backseat.

He demanded, "I'm still the director on or off the set. So don't you dare undermine my authority."

An hour later, he realized where "we" had goofed. After driving in continuous circles for miles, it turned out we were two miles away in the wrong city.

We never discussed the situation the next day at work, except at one point when we both happened to stop at the craft service table at the same time. He accidentally tipped the sugar jar over and watched it spill all over the table. Then he said to me, "Clean it up, PA."

It wasn't what he said but how he said it. I knew that in his own way he was trying to thank me for my kindness.

Directors Who Stink

I was an office PA with a prominent production company that was trying to woo Jane, a young up and coming director from Seattle. She had just completed her first edgy, underground film that was raising some eyebrows for its bold depiction of sex and youth.

The production company I was working at loved Jane so much that they offered me as her sacrificial chauffeur. I'll tell you something—she stunk.

I am not referring to her gritty noir filmmaking. No, she smelled so foul that I was forced to breathe out of my mouth with the windows open for the three days I drove her around town. Her aroma was similar to that of rotting produce mixed with an unsubtle hint of an outhouse. I had no idea a woman was capable of such stench.

Even though I was grossed out by her malodor, Jane was so much fun to hang out with. We had a lot in common as far as our family backgrounds and career aspirations. She was the epitome of fun from the way she dressed to the way she wore her hair (despite the glistening oil), to the funny things she'd say. After our first day together, she even treated me to a fancy dinner.

I wanted to know if it was just my nostrils or if everyone else could smell her. I didn't want to be overly critical about it. It was probably more in my head since I had been fixating on it all day. Once we got to the restaurant, I carefully gauged the maitre d's reaction to the peculiar aroma.

He definitely detected *something*. He even checked the bottom of his shoes before he discreetly sniffed me.

At dinner, I met some of Jane's interesting filmmaker friends. Her smell didn't seem to bother any of them, but they all had on pretty powerful perfumes and colognes. They came prepared.

The next day, Jane brought me along to every meeting she went to with agents and entertainment lawyers. I could see these people could smell it too. Some opened windows, others tried to cover their noses. I kept my chair as far away as possible and tried to sit upwind with every chance. I was getting embarrassed for her...and me. Every now and then I'd excuse myself to get a wet paper towel for my nose hoping people would realize the smell wasn't leaving with me.

I debated about whether I should tell Jane or not. Obviously none of her true friends had ever been honest enough with her. I thought, maybe I should be the one to say something or at least give her a nice bar of soap. Instead I took her to the perfume counter at the nearest department store and sprayed her with a few fragrances. She practically gagged and exclaimed loudly, "Ewww, puke-o. These smells are making me nauseous."

After our three fun filled days together, I was sad she had to go back home—but my lungs were going to implode if I didn't get rid of her quickly.

I rushed her to the airport (at about nine hundred miles an hour) and we said our good-byes. I was careful not to hug her too tightly as her oils might seep into my clothes. As soon as she left, I sprayed my car interior with some industrial strength disinfectant five times.

But it didn't help. Nothing could kill the noxious odor. I resigned myself to driving with my head hanging out my window.

Two weeks later I found a dirty sock of Jane's that had fallen out of her suitcase and was wedged under the passenger seat. The white sock had actually turned a disturbingly blue-green hue that matched my roommate's face when I waved it in front of her.

To this day, my car has never smelled like it did in the pre-Jane years.

In Search of the Tousand Dollar Pen

Maude was a PA on a hit television sitcom. One day the crew took the show outside of their usual stage and onto the backlot's grassy field. After a labored day of unusually tricky exterior shots, everyone went back to the production office to soothe his or her frazzled nerves. Because they had deviated from the semi-orderly confines of their stage, everyone was worried that things were forgotten.

The director was especially spooked by something. For an hour he walked around the production office trying to figure out which scene he hadn't shot. He reviewed the script; everything appeared to be in order. He reviewed the videotaped footage; it was all there. So what the heck was missing?

Uh oh, it was his pen. This wasn't any old Bic ballpoint we're talking about here. He had lost his one thousand dollar Mont Blanc pen. He started pacing the halls of the production office trying to recall the last place he saw it. Ah ha! He had loaned it to Maude only an hour prior.

The director told the producer. The producer freaked out and yelled at the production coordinator. The production coordinator shook his head and told his assistant. The assistant laughed and told Maude to scour the lot's acres of fields for the pricey pen *she* lost.

Maude knew full well she had returned the pen to the director. Unfortunately no one believed her. The director was taking a quiet moment alone so Maude couldn't *help remind* him he had lost his mind, too. She wondered how this man could have been so careless. Even worse, she wondered if she was going to have to pay for his mistake. She raced over to the grass as she clutched her overzealous heart. One thousand dollars? That was two month's worth of rent, plus a lot of groceries!

After a two hour fruitless search of intensely combing the grass on all fours, Maude, the ever devoted PA with a heart of gold and a wallet of copper, was forced to swallow her pride. She went back to the office with her head hung low, her pants full of grass stains, her elbows bloodied, and her fingernails crusty with dirt. She apologized to the production coordinator for not being able to find the director's pen that was worth more than her car. She bit down on her trembling lip with an empty feeling of utter failure as she waited for Fate's (in this case, the producer's) decision to be handed down to her.

The director overheard Maude's failed attempt to rescue the pen and he laughed, "Oh, I found that old pen a couple of hours ago. It was in my bag all along."

CHAPTER FOUR

Ac-turds

A ctors are a funny breed. Those who are dying to get their big break will treat you, the humble production assistant, with dire admiration and utter gratitude. These part-time waiters are the only ones on the set who are actually nice to production assistants. They are the only people on the job who seem to remember how to say those wonderful words we all crave to hear like 'please' and 'thank you.'

However, actors who are big—or worse, those who THINK they're big—are usually the biggest pains in the buttocks. These walking egomaniacs think they are the most important creatures on the set.

If I ruled the world, the first thing I would change (after I instated the five day weekend) is the hierarchical structure of Hollywood. Production Assistants would make a hundred times more money than the actors and the actors would have to get lunch for the PAs.

The Actor's Trailer, The Actor's Castle

It was my very first day ever on a movie set. I arrived bright and early at six in the morning having no idea what was in store for me. The production coordinator saw me trembling alone in the parking lot. He handed me a walkie talkie as if I had any clue how to use it. He told me to wait for the grips to arrive in the stake bed and have them park it in the back corner.

I just stood there with a look that basically said, "Huh?" I had no idea what a grip was and why they were delivering a lot of steaks. The production coordinator saw how inexperienced I was and assured me that everything was going to be okay. He told me to go relax, have breakfast and then make sure the trailers were clean for the actors when they arrived. All right, **this** I could handle.

I was so elated that they were feeding me for free, so I had to indulge myself by sampling all the delicacies. I was in college at the time so anything free and **not** dorm food was considered gourmet to me.

I cruised around the room meeting some of the crew. They were happy to see a new face on the set. I was ecstatic to talk to real movie people. After learning the difference between a grip and an electrician (a grip use an average of 127 profanities an hour while an electrician uses only about 126), I suddenly realized I had probably spent too much time chatting on my first day. I didn't want to look like a slacker, so I hurried over to the actors' trailers to make sure they were spotless.

Inside the biggest Winnebago with two side pop-outs, I found a nice woman. She looked so familiar but I couldn't figure out why. Nervously I introduced myself as I wiped down the kitchen table. I was trying to make conversation with my fellow co-worker but she wasn't responding to my small talk. She kept watching me as though I was a talking elephant. I figured she didn't speak English; so I asked her, "Do you speak English?"

She opened her mouth to say something but all she managed to get out was an "Uuughhh" sound. Yeah, I thought, she was just as nervous as I was.

I tried to make her feel better by saying, "Is it you're first day as a production assistant too? Here, why don't we have some fruit?" I offered the plate of food that I figured was conveniently on the kitchen table for anyone who got hungry.

"What are you doing in my trailer?" she barked in perfect English.

Aha! She was the delightful actress for whom this lovely trailer stood. My first lesson about actors was that they do NOT like uninvited guests barging into their trailers even if you're cleaning their counters and eating their breakfast.

Apologizing profusely, I ran out of there as she pelted me with an assortment of fresh fruit.

I went to the set to seek refuge. That lasted for about twelve seconds before the second assistant director handed me a Diet Coke to deliver to the make-up trailer immediately.

Guess who ordered the beverage. That's right, The Wicked Actress of the Westside. When I walked into the make-up trailer, she and the entire hair and make-up department turned to me with a glare that only hair and make-up people are capable of giving.

"That's the girl," howled the actress with a twisted evil laugh. They all cackled like witches and pointed at me. I handed over the Diet Coke and stumbled out of there before they boiled me in their cauldron. Their nefarious tittering continued until I was far out of earshot.

Throughout the rest of the longggggg day, the huge joke of the set was…me.

Where's my Coffee?

When a haughty, self-involved actor asks a non-coffee drinking production assistant to make him a cup of coffee, you know it is sheer death for that PA. My advice to anyone in this predicament is to run home to the safety of your mother as fast as you can. Do not attempt to fill the actor's request because you will, by definition of the Hollywood food chain, be shot down by the actor for not getting it right. Subsequently, you will suffer inevitable embarrassment in front of many of your peers.

You may think that theoretically you will be able to get the coffee the way that it has been described to you. But due to unknown forces, the coffee will turn out disastrous and the actor will complain like a two-year-old. Do not be surprised if the actor even blames you for the quality of the coffee beans that were picked in Columbia.

As a good (a.k.a. submissive) production assistant, you are required to humbly take responsibility for not only how the bean was picked and shipped to United States, but also how it was roasted by people in a different city.

I was one of those production assistants who naively thought I could beat the system.

"Get me a cup of coffee with a little milk," bellowed the actor. It seemed simple enough. It was a task I **knew** I could handle. I went to college for four years. I had been a Brownie and a Girl Scout. However, the actor might as well have asked me to bring him a unicorn.

Everyone was getting close to shooting the scene. The actor was getting his final touch-ups done by the make-up artist, so I placed the coffee (which I was confident was what he wanted) right next to him as I told him I was doing. He didn't bother to answer me because he was too busy being worked on. It's funny how actors seem to think it's "hard work" to have someone put make-up on them.

I repeated to him that his coffee was there.

Without opening his eyes, he said in a huff, "I'm not deaf. I heard you the first time."

The make-up woman gave me a sympathetic look as to say, 'he's always like this.'

When I walked away, I heard the actor say, "Who was that? This set is full of morons."

I was so glad I could help out such a kind and giving man. If only the audience, who would see him months later as a warm grandfather character, knew what a great human being he really was.

The assistant director called out, "last looks," indicating we were about to shoot. The actor took a sip of the coffee I placed beside him. His eyes spun inside his head and he spit the coffee onto the set's beautiful, white couch where the scene was about to take place. This got the entire crew's attention really fast.

"Who made this god-awful #^%!)@ coffee?" the actor hollered.

I didn't exactly do a backflip and announce that it was me. But, somehow the whole crew knew. Simultaneously eighty-nine people turned to look at me. Most of the faces staring at me were pretty sympathetic; except for the actor who thought I had set out to destroy him, and the set decorator who was hurriedly sopping up the wet brown mess on the couch.

The Egg White Omelet Adventures

Jack was a happy-go-lucky PA working on a big budget, big studio film. He was having such a good time, especially on this day because his favorite actress was shooting her cameo performance.

This mighty actress who's famous for making audiences shiver with sexual tension and executives quiver with fear, asked for an egg white omelet. Jack was happy to fetch the breakfast order for this beautiful woman whose entire collection of films he had seen dozens of times. He couldn't believe he was working this close to the sex goddess all day. He pushed his tongue back inside his mouth as he placed her order with the caterer.

When he delivered her the omelet, she screamed in a blood curdling shrill. Everyone in earshot hurried to her. The producer had his cell phone ready to call "Entertainment Tonight." The medic had her first aid supplies in hand.

The crew converged in front of the actress who was holding her omelet at arm's length as if it were a beating heart.

"My God, what's wrong?" dramatically asked the producer.

"There's…there's…," she choked. The medic was getting in place to perform the Heimlich Maneuver on her.

"There's a speck of yolk in my omelet!" the actress screamed. "Get me another, and make it *right* this time!"

Jack hopped to attention and ran to the caterer to take care of this matter. He carefully oversaw the caterer remake the order. This time Jack and the caterer were both positive the actress had nothing to complain about.

Jack presented the actress with the pure virgin white egg omelet. Again, she refused it insisting he was trying to sabotage her body with fat and cholesterol. She threatened to have Jack fired, dismembered, and worst of all—banned from Hollywood forever. Could one woman have that power? Jack did not want to test her.

The actress turned to the other PA, Jenna, who was standing nearby trying to discreetly eavesdrop. She snarled at Jenna to get her a new egg white omelet and this time have it cooked in a copper frying pan. Then she told Jenna to hurry it up because after all, she was famished!

As Jenna and Jack went to the caterer, they suddenly had an idea. They refused to let this woman waste anymore embryos. The two hid behind the catering truck for a couple of moments. Then Jenna smugly brought over the exact same omelet to the actress. The beastly thespian took one bite and moaned in sheer ecstasy at its exquisite taste. After two tiny, micro-sized bites, she discarded the food saying she was absolutely stuffed and needed to purge.

Air Conditioner Boy

It's a widely known fact in Tinsel Town that the "talent" is not superhuman. The truth is that major celebrities put on one pant leg at a time—even though it's usually one lavishly expensive Armani pant leg (over outrageously pricey undies) at a time. However, no matter how many big-eyed kids and sex-crazed fans idolize some over-paid hot shot, stars are simply flesh and bones who are hypersensitive to extreme weather conditions.

Try being around any given tantrum-potential talent on a midsummer afternoon in the San Fernando Valley and you will see an over-exaggerated case of Hollywood irritability rear its ugliest head. Forget the eighty-five other crew members and insignificant nobody co-stars with bodies melting under the toasty ozone-challenged Southern California sun. If there is the American equivalent to royalty perspiring in his or her costume, there's going to be trouble!

On one high budget movie, the heat was unbearable at the downtown courthouse location. While everyone was frying at the one hundred plus temperatures, a certain actor demanded he be kept chilled at a reasonable 61.7 degrees between takes. He actually had a lawyer on retainer to make sure this clause was in all of his contracts. If the producers had not respected the actor's wishes to be kept on ice, he would have refused to "act."

Whatever happened to the thespians who lived and died for their *craft?*

When Cameron started as a PA on this film, he got in good with the electricians. They all just sort of clicked. He found himself helping them out with cords and insulator tubing and all that sort of fun stuff. Because of his high-tech know how of plugging things into outlets, he was the producer's number one pick to blow air on the actor when commanded.

If Cameron were a comic book action hero, he would be shown in all his stunning glory waving his giant, floppy, yellow air duct while wearing a spiffy cape. He would be called Air Conditioner Boy. Or as he was affectionately referred to by the actor—"that #%$-ing air conditioner boy."

And that was Cameron's job for the entire film whether they were on the set or on location. I know what you're thinking. Why can't *I* have a job that easy?

Buyer beware. According to Cameron, that kind of job requires much more effort than you can imagine. It is absolutely vital to not only read the actor's mind, but be able to eyeball the actor's temperature discomfort. You must become one with the actor's skin color. Or at least be able to flick the "on" switch before you get yelled at.

Lions, Tigers, and Boobs—Oh My

Samantha was a sweet and innocent rose-scented production assistant on the set of a cheesy, low budget, bordering-on-soft-porn film. She was befriended by the beautifully fresh supporting actress named Cindy. It was both of their first times working on a film. It was also each of their first times being so far from home.

Samantha started out as Cindy's driver and their relationship quickly blossomed into a friendship between the two Midwesterners. After a couple of weeks, the two young, moralistic women became inseparable. In a way, they were forced to keep each other safe from the strange people on the crew and the even stranger working conditions.

Both women came from families who supported their struggling Hollywood careers. However, neither of the women had expected to work on anything so vulgar as this movie. But, they had come so far for this opportunity that they weren't about to blow their chances—no matter how nauseating those chances were.

These two country bumpkins quickly got a full-fledged lesson on life in Los Angeles. Everyday they were tested mentally and morally by this film. For Samantha it was tasks like going into adult shops to pick up dental floss-sized costumes and massage oils. For Cindy, it was repeated requests from the slimy, old director to reveal just a wee bit more skin during each take.

Both women were repulsed by the indecency of it all. They spent many a night shedding tears together worrying that this would be the extent of their careers. They were so scared they'd never fulfill their dreams of being rich and famous Hollywood players and would have to work at McDonald's—or worse, work in [screeching violins, please] an OFFICE.

What they really wanted was to break out and do studio feature films. The kind of movies where actors were fully clothed. The kind of shows where PAs worked for respectable producers who didn't walk around with their shirts unbuttoned exposing their gold chains against their hairy chests.

Until they could meet people around town who would give them such fulfilling work, Samantha and Cindy kept plugging away at this demoralizing trash. But hey, it paid the psychiatrist bills.

No matter how crude it all got, Samantha was proud of her new friend for keeping her head on straight and not giving into the director's demands to reveal more flesh on…and off…the set.

Before long, Samantha and Cindy were loosening up. They began to see the humor in everything. After all, how many people had bosses who were desperately trying to join the Mafia but couldn't find any mobsters who'd hang out with them?

Although neither of the women were about to compromise their principles, they started to fit into the Hollywood lifestyle a little more easily. Samantha even started to see Cindy using the surrounding opportunities to her advantage.

She noticed Cindy spending more time with the director in order to "learn as much about show business as he could teach her." Samantha still wasn't comfortable around the director in general but figured it was good for Cindy as long as she knew what she was doing.

On the last day of filming, after Cindy had wrapped, she asked Samantha to drive her someplace as quickly as possible. However, she was very secretive about where she wanted to go. Samantha's curiosity was killing her as Cindy directed her through West Hollywood.

They finally pulled up to a hospital. Samantha gasped with fear. "Are you alright? Did the director…" she quivered with fear that the dirty old man had done something horrible to Cindy.

"Yes," Cindy admitted. "How did you know?"

"What did he do to you?" Samantha asked with balled up fists.

"He's paying for my boob job. Want to come in with me and watch?" Cindy asked gleefully. Samantha politely declined and left her friend to acclimate herself with Los Angeles' most precious commodity—plastic surgery.

That was the last time Samantha and Cindy spoke to each other. Samantha is now an assistant production coordinator for a commercial production company. Last she heard, Cindy was headlining at a "highly respectable" club three times a day by the LAX Airport. She was supposedly going by the name Candy Mams.

The Smoking Stack

Everyone in Hollywood smokes. Everyone. Even animal actors can be found behind the stage lighting up. So what if you go into Hollywood with virgin pink lungs? You gotta learn to puff it, baby.

Oh not me, you say to yourself. I won't fall prey to neurotic quirks just to be cool and fit in. That's what Selia said before she met a certain actress who smoked a pack a day—and that was on a good hair day with no bloating.

No, it wasn't that the actress drove Selia to smoke with her wild demands and deranged personality disorders; though God knows that actress had plenty to go around for the entire planet. No, this actress had a truly bizarre quirk that out did all of her other eccentricities—she would never start her own cigarette. She believed it was bad luck. One of her gurus told her that.

Selia should never have had to deal with this odd thespian further than being a "gofer" (as in "go-fer my coffee") because the actress had a personal assistant to do all her dirty work. However, on this fine occasion, the actress' personal assistant/cigarette starter was out because of a relative's death.

To understand this actress is to know what she said to her grieving assistant's news of taking a few days off. The actress compassionately asked, "Do you really have to go? It's not like you were **that** friggin' close to your grandmother."

Unfortunately for Selia, the actress' sympathetic tactic did not keep the personal assistant from hopping on the first flight out of town.

"Now who's going to smoke my Virginias?" whined the actress as she locked eyes on the young, pristine, taught-skinned twenty-three-year-old PA. Selia tried to escape, but this actress had the radar of a smart bomb and was locked on target.

Selia made it clear she did not smoke anything, not even wimpy sucker sticks that have come a long way, baby.

"Yes you do," the evil temptress vehemently uttered in a nicotine-deprived whisper.

"But—," Selia desperately protested as the mother ship pulled her closer.

"You'll do it because I said so," the actress commanded.

"No!" Selia shook her head and sternly wagged her finger at the actress.

"I'll pay you a hundred dollars a day," the actress quipped.

Sold to the non-smoker in the back for a hundred dollars!

"But only this once," sneered Selia. She really liked money.

"Okay, you smoke it to this point." The dramatist took a red pen to every cigarette in the pack intricately drawing a thin line three quarters of the way up the cigarettes. "Then I will take it from there."

One pack and a hundred tax-free dollars later, Selia was sick to her stomach. But damn it, the money was good, she thought as she threw up in the actress' mobile home toilet.

Big foot's revenge

Jessica was a production assistant on a television movie of the week. She was slightly heavier than your average rail thin, silicone enhanced LA'lien. Because of her "less than perfect" measurements, she was hand picked by the show's actress to be her workout inspiration.

Jessica was humiliated and utterly repulsed at the suggestion. She would rather cut out her tongue than be subjected to such harsh degradation by an egomaniac with an inferiority complex.

The starlet was angry at being turned down, but she refused to give up. She offered Jessica an enticing sum of bribe money along with the glory of working out with the self-titled Goddess of Goodness.

Jessica would not allow herself to be debased and walked away from the proposition. She was about to walk off the show completely when the actress upped the ante to a very robust deal. We're talking lots of green bills!

Jessica thought about it, carefully weighed both sides of this mess, and decided not to be a fool. What the hell! She'd take the offer which meant that for two hours a day she would sweat with the actress and a trainer. The rest of her day would be spent running around like usual for the production company. In essence, she'd be doubling her money with no extra hours and gaining free access to the world's best gym equipment.

This was fantastic despite the moral dissatisfaction that lingered with Jessica for weeks. That is, only until she won a part in the show—a body part. You see, the actress was so sickly obsessed about looking perfect, she freaked out when the director added a bare foot scene into the script. The actress refused to allow the public to see her feet that were full of bunions and a nasty fungal infection.

In an effort to save her flawless reputation, the actress demanded they use a foot double. She suggested Jessica's beautifully manicured and handsomely shaped footsies would work perfectly.

The actress yanked and poked at Jessica as she scrupulously inspected the bare feet she would have America believe were hers. Despite the actress' foot fetish, Jessica finally agreed to be her foot double when the actress added a little more bribe money to the pot.

The director was taking shot after shot of Jessica's comely bare feet walking through the grass. The director thought she was a natural and suggested she do this for a living. Jessica was enjoying her moment in the sun. All the while, the actress was watching from the sidelines and turning green with envy.

The next day at their regular workout time, the actress excused Jessica from exercising with her any further. Actually she told Jessica, "Get out of my gym, you cheap wanna-be. You can never be as good as me, feet or no feet."

Alright, so the actress had some issues. Jessica smiled about it all the way to the car dealership where she put a handsome down payment on her brand new car.

Happy, Dopey, Sleepy...

Reed was a well educated, polite young man who aspired to direct feature films someday. As a PA on a racy independent film, his assignment was to look after the leading man. It seemed like an easy task, especially because the actor wasn't *that* well known.

This overseas entertainer had recently moved to the States in pursuit of becoming the superstar he is today. But even then, this foreigner was a wild man and Reed soon discovered his job was not as easy as he originally thought.

Everyday Reed would greet the actor with a respectful, "Good morning, sir. What can I get you for breakfast?"

The response changed from day to day with this guy. Sometimes he would order something, other times he would throw a shoe at Reed's head indicating he'd be passing on food that morning. There was actually an indentation on the trailer door from the semi-regular thwacking it took. Fortunately for Reed, the actor's aim wasn't too good. It was the verbal abuse that hurt more.

With his international schooling, the actor had an eloquent command of the English language. He took great pleasure in using his intelligence to berate anyone he felt worthy. Thanks to his background in Psychology, the actor also had an insightful gift of cutting people to the core. He'd regularly take aim at various people on the set and rip them apart with insults. One day, he successfully cleared the lunch tent with his ruthless racism.

Reed and the actor were hardly friends, but some days the actor would break down his tough-man act and open up to Reed. They could shoot the breeze for hours—or at least the actor could while Reed tried to keep himself from keeling over in boredom.

Whether he wanted to or not, Reed learned how stressful it was to be the up and coming actor of the hour. He got an earful of how everyone wanted a piece of the actor; how old girlfriends were trying to rekindle the flame in order to get tabloid worthy dirt on him; how friends were constantly asking for favors and money. There was so much pressure on the actor to be perfect. And according to him, there was no margin of error for him on this film. It was either going to catapult him into stardom or ruin his shine for good.

Reed thought he was laying it on a little thick, but after all, drama was his gift. He sympathized with the thespian a little bit and admired his honesty. However, that was as far as their relationship went. Generally, after the actor spent time crying on Reed's shoulder, he would turn around and yell at Reed to get lost.

Near the end of the two-month shoot, the tension was rising. Everyone wanted to kill the actor after he spit his dinner out all over the caterer. Each day got worse as the actor got more infuriated with everything from the director's directing to the actress' acting to the wardrobe he had to wear.

The crew looked to Reed for some answers. They wanted him to figure out how to keep the star happy, or at least restrained. His erratic behavior was costing them time and money and was ruining the film.

Unfortunately, Reed could offer them no solutions. It seemed the only time this actor was ever truly nice and seemingly happy was when his buddy came to visit. No one knew who this friend was. He would just kind of show up, visit the actor in his trailer for a few minutes and leave.

One night, without any provocation, the actor started going crazy. The director commanded everyone to take a twenty minute break. Reed was told to wait outside the actor's trailer for fear of what the actor would do if left alone.

Reed obliged and stood outside in a quarterback stance ready for anything the actor could throw his way. Suddenly the actor's buddy came by, smiled at Reed, and went inside the trailer without knocking. After a few silent moments, the guy came out and nodded goodbye to Reed. Reed watched the mysterious man walk away.

A couple of minutes passed and Reed gingerly knocked on the actor's trailer door. A sweet voice chimed, "Yes?" Reed wondered if there was someone else in the trailer.

The door opened slowly as if by someone savoring the first sight and smell of the outdoors. Out came the actor…with a white powder ring around his nostril. Sadly, all Reed could do was hand him a tissue as they headed back towards the set.

CHAPTER FIVE

Producers Who Should Be Banished from the Biz

Believe it or not, there is a breed of incompetents in this business who somehow snuck through the barricades of Hollywood politics. Or, perhaps they were ushered through these same barricades because of those politics.

Someone somewhere thought it would be a good idea to garnish these people with a "Producer" title (or *Producicorus Idiotica*) and give them free run "producing" a film. The problem is *someone* forgot to teach these people what the hell "producing" meant. Don't get me wrong, not all producers are morons—just the ones who try so hard convincing everyone they know what they're doing.

Although no one can accurately define *what* a producer does, everyone can always tell *who* the producer is on the set by his or her distinct characteristics. For example, this unique breed of *Producicorus Idiotica* can be easily recognized by their protruding egos and need to talk on a cellular phone for hours at a time. They can usually be spotted sitting in their director chairs with their names embroidered nice and obvious on the back. They are generally demanding yellers with annoyed looks on their faces all day. These strange creatures enjoy throwing around unreasonable commands pretending they're "producing" even though they have no clue what's really going on.

Do not become alarmed when I tell you that they are actually aliens from the planet Duh.

The Twilight Zone

I once worked for one of these aliens—a producer named Yvonne. She was so high on her exemplary bossy title that she neglected to realize the insignificance of this silly little short film we were making. No one was ever going to see it, except maybe relatives. I didn't care though. It was my chance to meet new contacts.

My first job of the morning was to greet the crew in the parking lot and make sure they parked within the white lines. A zippy sports car whizzed past me, stopped short and squealed into reverse clearing me only by millimeters. It was Yvonne. I could imagine her as a child in school. She probably stole every little girl's Barbie and ripped off the heads.

She took a moment to size me up with her shifty eyes and started throwing all sorts of information at me. Realize that at this point, I didn't even know her name. She didn't have time for such mundane pleasantries like greetings.

She smacked her gum loudly and ordered me to go to her Manhattan Beach home, which was close to a gazillion miles away from the Malibu stage, and pick up her puppy. Not being very fond of dogs, I told her it was my policy not to transport animals in my car.

"Oh it's just a puppy dog," she cooed. Then she glared at me as if to say that my job depended on picking up her dog. Actually she said, "Your job depends on picking up my dog."

Then she rudely "asked" if I could put a rush on it! Aliens from the planet Duh are best known for their need of immediacy on **everything**. Example dialogue: "I need a low-fat graham cracker with a paper thin spread of peanut butter on the back for my taste buds to enjoy—STAT!"

I was about to go pick up the pup when she said, "Oh by the way…"

Everyone knows this kind of person who always has a few extra little favors to ask of you, you know, "while you're at it." And of course those "by the way, few little extra things" are never, ever, ever little.

She pulled out a list of things she wanted me to bring back. It was longer than Ted Kacynzski's manifesto.

She **had** to have her sunglasses, sunscreen, fingernail polish, a toothbrush, her favorite pillow…

I figured I would just throw in a couple of doorknobs while I was at it. Then she told me to swing by a special drug store near her house to pick up her desperately needed prescription. After she was finished speaking to me as if I had the intelligence of a street lamp, she burned rubber leaving me to choke in her car exhaust.

Excuse me, but why hadn't she brought all of this junk with her when she left her house this morning? I was about to take this issue up with her, but she was already too busy yelling at the stage manager she nearly ran over for not getting out of her way fast enough. This woman sure knew how to start a day off right!

At that point I would have gone anywhere to get myself away from this disgustingly arrogant, obnoxiously loud, disturbingly suntanned woman with a bad permanent for at least a little while.

After a really, really long drive, I got to Yvonne's beach house to find her puppy. Puppy my foot! It was a HUGE, hairy golden retriever. This furry, saliva-dripping beast on four legs was Chewbacca on steroids. Its immediate reaction was to slime me with drool. During a ten minute standoff, I tried to show the monster who was boss.

I guess technically, the dog won. It was standing on top of me while I was sprawled on the floor protecting my face from liquid debris. Because I was protecting my face and eyes, I couldn't see the source of the drizzle. I could only pray that the hyperactive creature had already been housebroken!

As much fun at this was, I had to go pick up her **important** prescription. I must admit I was a little worried. I hate to see anyone ill or in pain.

The pharmacist was a cute old man who liked to talk. So much so that for twenty minutes he lectured me on how Yvonne was supposed to apply this acne medicine. Emergency ACNE MEDICINE?!

Back at the beach house, I was greeted with a friendly gesture of muddy paws all over me from that all too happy, hairy fiend. I pulled a blanket from Yvonne's abominably unkempt bedroom floor so the dog's claws wouldn't ruin my backseat. The puppy was more than happy to go on a road trip, but first he had to inspect my entire car. I tried to reason with the animal to sit still for the forty-minute drive. I even tried communicating telepathically. I had to face facts—this pup did not understand the concept of keeping within his limitations of the blanket.

After jumping and barking for the first fifteen miles of our trip, he decided he'd be more comfortable lounged across the front seats drooling and farting. Guess which end I got.

When I got back to the stage, Yvonne was so happy to see her dog and her acne medicine that she didn't pay me any attention. That is, not until I handed her the blanket that was in the backseat. It turned out to be Yvonne's recently deceased grandmother's old blanket that had been in the family for like twelve generations. She started turning a frightening yellowish purple while her eyes became beet red.

How does one apologize for something like that? Fortunately, the dog did not destroy the antique blanket because he was too busy chewing my passenger seat headrest.

Later that day, I saw the way Yvonne doted upon her pooch. Maybe I wasn't giving her the credit and respect she deserved. Maybe she wasn't as crude as I thought. Obviously her dog really liked her. Perhaps she even knew how to produce a film very well. Who was I to judge anyone?

I decided to give our relationship another chance, so I sat next to her at lunch. A few other PAs joined us and soon we got into a conversation about vegetarianism. This was promising. We were finally communicating at a human level about an interesting topic. Yvonne asked me my views on the topic. I explained how I emphatically did not and will never eat meat.

The next thing I knew, she was chasing me around the room with handfuls of pepperoni, laughing maniacally. The other PAs watched in shock at this display of madness. This woman belonged in an insane asylum. Forget any contacts she may have been able to provide me with, I just wanted to get out of there with my life and without meat products flying on me.

The Coffee Brigade

There once was a young independent film producer who was barely making ends meet. This was a man willing to risk it all for his art. He once said he'd rather die than compromise his cinematic ideals for Hollywood's blood money.

One hit, no-budget, where-did-that-come-from film later, he became a huge international success. Without a second thought, he changed his poor maverick filmmaker tune for the fat Hollywood paycheck faster than a roach can run. A big studio wooed him into a sweet housekeeping, three-picture deal where he was furnished with a lavish office complete with antiques, a fully stocked kitchen, free phone calls, free postage, and a staff of four.

That's when his ego skyrocketed to infinite proportions and his drinking problem began. It was actually a coffee-drinking problem and Gerald, the twenty-three-year-old office PA, was the unfortunate victim of it all.

Each morning started out exactly the same with the producer rushing into the office where Gerald greeted this man with a heartfelt "good morning, sir."

The producer, who was only five years Gerald's senior, gave Gerald nothing more than a grunt in return as he stormed into his office. The producer felt he was above all that nice, polite crap since he was, after all, a huge international success.

After the producer's grand entrance, Gerald would wait three minutes and, just like clockwork, the producer would yell for his coffee. Gerald was prepared for this request as well as the producer's quintessential reaction. This man was so picky that even after two months of constantly demanding all sorts of coffee, he still could not find a brand or flavor he enjoyed.

He complained that Starbucks was too strong, Pete's was too rich, the corner coffee shop was not enough of a status symbol, etc.

Everyday Gerald had a new kind of exotic blend for him but nothing satisfied this producer when it came to java.

One might think the producer would have stopped trying so hard and just picked a new beverage. Nope, he insisted on following the coffee craze like all of his cool, new Hollywood friends. He was so concerned about being hip that he even went to Alcoholics Anonymous to fit in with the Tinsel Town lifestyle—despite the fact that he didn't drink.

Regardless, each day Gerald prayed that by some miracle he could make the producer happy. There was more at stake here for Gerald than job security. You see, instead of disposing the undesired coffee properly, the young, disrespectful producer would spit his coffee out on Gerald.

In the hopes of saving himself and his clothes from the line of fire, Gerald desperately went out in search of "good" coffee. One day he went into a local no-name market that smelled of mildew and bug spray and picked up a can of grounds packaged in bright generic yellow.

The next morning went according to routine until the producer sipped the new coffee. Gerald waited for the scalding waterworks, but this time there were none.

Both men's eyes grew large with merriment. For the very first time, Gerald saw the producer smile. It was more like a painful smirk but there was definitely love in the room that day.

For three months this bliss continued. Everyone in the office was instructed, by threat of decapitation, to keep the generic coffee a secret. If the producer knew, he was drinking the uncoolest brand in the world, heads would have rolled.

The biggest problem arose when the filthy little mom and pop store that carried the coffee disappeared into out-of-business heaven. No one else in town sold the generic grounds and Gerald knew he'd be dead meat if he didn't keep the supply coming.

It took him an entire week of early mornings and late nights to hunt down the manufacturer, but Gerald was not a quitter. He ended up finding their headquarters in the middle of nowhere Michigan.

With only a handful of grounds left in the can and he himself teetering on the verge of a heart attack, Gerald successfully secured a steady supply of the coffee by the mega-pounds.

To perpetuate the secret, every time a coffee shipment arrived at the office, Gerald had to intercept the deliveryman in the hall and grab the hideously loud, neon yellow cans. Once he snuck the goods into glass jars, he had to drive over to a dumpster located at the far end of the lot to dispose of the evidence.

This carried on for two more months until one day the producer realized that his circle of friends were giving up coffee and moving on to teas. They claimed tea "opened the mind to creativity." Soon after he quit coffee, the producer enrolled in Yoga classes on the advice of his new therapist/girlfriend.

You can imagine how thrilled Gerald was to start this process all over again.

Jane, Dick, & Harry

See Jane, the producer, speed. See Dick, the cop, pull Jane over. See Jane yell, scream, and berate Dick. See Dick enjoy giving Jane a hefty ticket for speeding, having an expired license and too many outstanding parking tickets. See Jane take her frustrations out on Harry, the office production assistant. See Harry be sad for having to keep his crappy job.

To say the least, Jane was a major pain in the butt to everyone who knew her. She was even worse to those who worked for her. To her, employees were mere disposable commodities only alive to serve her. Her thoughts on husbands were pretty much the same. She seemed to go through both quicker than Power Bars.

Harry had worked for Jane for a miserable five months. Every night he dreamed of causing her physical injury. However, with great difficulty, he resisted the daily temptation.

After Jane returned from her personal Indie 500 race on the 405 freeway, she continued her highly dramatic frustration right on into the office. Within five minutes of walking in, she had her assistant in tears and had told her man du jour that she was breaking off their relationship. That was nothing compared to what she was like on Mondays after one of her films opened to a horrible weekend box office!

When Harry heard Jane stomp in the office, he took cover in the copy room.

"Where's Harry?" Jane shrieked. Harry tried to duck behind the copy machine but before he could fit himself behind the heavy mechanism that was pressed tight against the wall, he felt her piercing eyes watching him.

Without saying a word, she pointed him over to her. She was standing only five feet away but she refused to walk inside the icky copy room she endearingly referred to as the "servants' quarters."

Beleaguered at being found, Harry sheepishly walked over to her as if he was going to get a whacking on the knuckles with a ruler. Instead of assaulting him, she threw her newly acquired moving violation at her boy-slave.

"Here," she huffed curtly. "Go fight this at the courthouse for me. I was…I was…tell them I was sexually harassed by a cop. Don't get the press involved. I'll talk to my publicist about that later."

The very next day, Harry was at the courthouse with the representatives of Los Angeles County's vagrant, hoodlum, and prostitute populations. He sat next to a man who was drooling brown stuff for close to an hour while he waited for someone to call his name. Harry had no idea what the hell he was doing or where he was supposed to go, but he figured he'd rather sit next to someone who smelled like cow manure than be back at the office with She-Devil.

After about an hour and a half, Harry was directed to a line that was approximately the length of the Great Wall of China. When he finally reached the counter, he was greeted by an androgynous human thing stuffed inside its outfit like a sausage. It looked Harry over with a scowl, looked at the ticket he placed on the counter, then looked back at Harry with the same scowl.

"What the hell is this?" the being droned lacking the least bit of personality.

"I need to fight this. There was sexual harassment involved," Harry mumbled, having lost all the humor he once saw in this ridiculous nuisance.

The sausage person glared at the ticket and said to him, "Look Miss Jane, unless you show me I.D. to prove that you're even a woman, you've been standing in the wrong line. You've got to arrange a court date by calling the number on the back. Or I suggest you face facts, admit you're guilty, and pay the damn fine. As far as the expired registration goes, you need to take that up with the DMV."

Harry did not want to go back to the office with this information. It wasn't rocket science to figure out what Jane's reaction would be.

Instead of facing her, he decided to call from the courthouse and break the bad news over the telephone so she couldn't hit him.

Jane's initial retort was to curse Harry out. Then she became more rational and decided to bring her lawyer into this. She was incapable of making anything lack a full dose of extra-strength drama.

"Hurry back so you can meet with my lawyer and tell him your side of this story. He'll be interested in how they mistreated you at that courthouse and how you were afraid for your life," Jane coached.

See Harry go catch an afternoon matinee. See Jane become so self-involved that she doesn't even notice. See Jane's lawyer take care of the problem and gouge Jane for a ton of legal expenses. See Jane hide the cost within her next film's budget.

This is War

Max and Manny were a team. Everyone loved them and they were always the life of the party. Even back in kindergarten, the two of them were the class clowns. The teacher would constantly send them outside "to think about what they had done." Sure, they'd think about it, and then they'd come up with better material for next time.

This time the two were working as PAs on a micro-budget, non-union film. The pay was lousy but the crew was promised a strict schedule of twelve hour **maximum** days—which was (surprise, surprise) adhered to.

Everything about this film was unbelievably fantastic. The script was phenomenal, the cast was outstanding, and the crew was absolutely spectacular. There wasn't a single attitude to be found among the bunch and the cast and crew bonded quickly.

Then two weeks into the shoot, Max and Manny were told to clear the parking lot for three enormous trailers. Inside these super duper mobile homes were every amenity imaginable, including state of the art entertainment centers and fully stocked humidors with the world's fattest cigars. They discovered they were for the three older, wealthy executive producers who no one on the crew knew existed. It turned out, these men had come to spy on their investment and make sure they were getting the most work for their money.

Max and Manny knew the crew was in trouble just by looking at these curmudgeons' haughty Italian suits and horrible toupees. The first thing these weasels did was fire the film's producer who had originated the twelve hour workday policy.

The mood on the set changed instantly from happy-go-lucky and productive to heavy and frustrated. The executive producers immediately started putting restrictions on everything from petty cash allotments, to phone usage, to time spent in the bathroom.

People were getting resentful but no one wished to jeopardize the quality or completion of this potential award-worthy film by making waves.

The work hours started to drag out longer each night. The crew was getting increasingly hungry and irritable hours after lunch. Despite lengthening the crew's days, the executive producers opted not to provide them with additional meals.

Max and Manny really started to hate these old farts. First of all, the deluxe trailers were way out of line. Even the four actors had to share one smelly, cramped Winnebego that was barely tall enough for them to stand up straight. But even worse, Max and Manny could hear the old men bellyaching over how stupid the crew was and how they weren't getting everything done on time.

Max and Manny were getting upset. How upset were they? Let's just say that disgruntled postal workers have nothing on two angry production assistants with creative minds.

The next evening was an all-night shoot outside a house in a low-income neighborhood in East Los Angeles. These kinds of neighborhoods are a Mecca for evil producers because the neighbors usually don't speak much English and have no idea of the rules by which a film crew must abide. Therefore, complaints are almost never reported from these folks.

Thanks to Max and Manny's knowledge of the California State laws governing production companies, broken rules were not going to go unreported *that* evening.

At one in the morning, Max and Manny anonymously called the police to complain of noise. The cops promptly arrived demanding to see a filming permit. The executive producers went into a full-fledged tizzy. They started pulling out each other's hair from the bad toupees because they could not show a permit. Actually, they never applied for a permit because they were too cheap.

The police shut down production early that night. The next day the film permit office reviewed their budget and discovered it was too high for them to claim non-union status. Within moments, the union leaders were all over the three bald men like vultures on roadkill. Max and Manny kept a watchful eye on the situation (and an ear up to the trailer door) as the union folks "convinced" the men to change their ways.

After what seemed like a hundred years, the three executive producers came out of the trailer looking like they lost a few rounds to Mike Tyson's sexual advances. As a result, the executive producers were forced to raise their budget in order to pay **everyone** union scale wages.

This delighted Max and Manny who later went on to become a comedy writing and producing team. I am happy to note that they treat their staff very well and never ever allow their employees to work longer than nine hours a day.

Take Two of These and Don't Ever Call Me Again

It had been a long, hot, smoggy spring Friday in San Fernando Valley. Inside a sound stage, sitcom magic was happening and Francine, the PA, was soaking it all in. Actually, her clothes were soaking up all of her sweat.

Outside, the temperatures were finally dipping into the cooler 90's but the inside of the stage still felt like a pizza oven. It was getting late and Francine was looking forward to getting home to a nice cool shower. For her, it had been a typical overly hectic day that was exacerbated by the kind of weather that makes people want to go out on the freeways with semi-automatic weapons.

All day long she was either running around town picking up lunches and last minute props, avoiding accidents with road enraged drivers, pleading with meter maids not to ticket her car, or contending with a cranky audience who had waited in the broiling sun for hours.

But the chaos all finally came to an end when another episode was successfully "in the can." The live studio audience filed out of the stage easily enough, the set was cleaned up, and other crew members were going home. She felt her work here was complete for the week.

Francine was eagerly awaiting her routine dismissal by one of the producers. It had been a demeaning formality every single Friday for almost an entire season. But every week, Francine and a producer had to go through a checklist before she could be released like a prisoner.

Her favorite producer Devlin, who usually let her go each Friday without much of a fuss, happened to be out that day. She looked around for another friendly producer to dismiss her. She found all the remaining producers, those who hadn't high-tailed it out of there right after the curtain call, were busy schmoozing with the lingering agents and talent.

She looked at her watch and realized she was going to be able to get home at a relatively decent hour this evening—before midnight. Suddenly her aim became more focused on tracking down a producer to let her leave—now!

She finally found one of the producers and politely asked if there was anything more she could do before she took off. Ted, the painfully depraved producer, looked at his watch and saw that Francine still had an hour and a half to fulfill her twelve-hour workday. He reminded

Francine of her doctor's appointment that morning for which she came in two hours late.

How could he hold that against her? She worked her butt off every-day for this company. She had spent many nights pulling in overtime without any compensation—not even a thank you. And this was how they repaid her?!

She kept quiet though because she knew Ted had it out for her because…well, just because he could. After a brief pause, Ted snidely said, "I'll let you know when I need you."

Frustrated to the point of near rage, Francine went back to the empty office and tried to make the best of her time by getting some rest on the couch. Obviously there was nothing left to do that night, but at least she could get in a few winks.

Five minutes before her twelve hours were up, Francine gathered her things. Just as she was putting on her coat, Ted barged into the office and claimed, "Okay, I need you now."

What?! What could be so urgent at this hour?

"The executive producer needs you to pick up some aspirin right away and drop it off at his house," he announced with a glint of amuse-ment in his sunken eyes.

"But I'm going home," explained Francine as her eyes glassed over.

"Exactly. Drop it off on your way home. You both live on the Westside. It'll be perfect."

Yeah, perfect for the producer who was skipping out the door to go home to his exercise equipment and amphetamines.

Francine looked up the executive producer's address. Oh sure he lived on the same side of Los Angeles County as she did, but his house was basically as close to her apartment as Hawaii is to Japan.

She went to the nearest drug store and bought every kind of aspirin on the shelf. She wasn't about to get to this guy's house only to find he wanted tablets, not capsules. She'd been down *that* road too many times. When she was done, she had spent sixty dollars.

The minutes ticked on and her eyes grew heavier. She made her way around the winding roads of Pacific Palisades' elite neighborhoods with the radio blasting and cranked the busted air conditioner pretending her eleven-year-old car could chill below 89°.

According to the map, she was getting really close. Good, because her bed was calling out to her. At that point, she forgot all about the shower. She'd be lucky if she even made it to her front door without passing out on her welcome mat.

As she crept toward the executive producer's house, she passed a 7-Eleven, Vons, Savon, and Longs. What a great place to live, she thought to herself. Wouldn't it be so convenient to be surrounded by all these wonderful drug stores that were only a few blocks from this guy's house?

Her tiredness quickly turned into anger. Her eyes began to burn. She was ready to throw the medication at the executive producer's front lawn and keep going.

When she arrived at the multi-million dollar home, she had no idea what to expect. She hoped he was near death. She hoped he had coughed up a lung. She hoped he was so miserable that he couldn't sleep.

She knocked on the door grinding her teeth in frustration. The door opened and there was the show's head honcho standing there in an elegant smoking jacket with a tissue in his hand and a big smile on his face.

"What are you doing here Francine?" he said with a genuine happiness to see her. "You came all this way at this hour to bring me medicine? Aren't you the sweetest thing in the world."

Francine took one of the bottles of aspirin back for herself. She figured Ted would need it when she whacked him silly with a sledgehammer on Monday morning.

A Special Surprise

As a production assistant on a never-to-this-day-released film, I was promised that my cellular phone bill would be reimbursed in full for all work-related calls. I was only one of four people on the set to have a production cell phone. The other three belonged to the director and the two producers. No one bothered to ask those guys for phone privileges. The director was so afraid of germs that he didn't even like it when people breathed on him, let alone got their saliva near his thrice-daily disinfected phone. And the two anal-retentive producers who scrutinized every nickel and dime spent on the production were known to clock people's coffee breaks with a stopwatch.

It didn't take long for the crew to figure out I was the easiest target for free phone time. People would hunt me down and demand to use my phone as if their lives depended on it. I was a dealer to these cellular junkies and I couldn't tell them no. However, they were slowly racking up a small cellular fortune on my account.

I felt a little uneasy with all these expenses rampantly accruing on my bill. But, the production manager, the accountant and the line producer all assured me I would be paid back in full. In other words: "Shut up and let us use your phone."

A couple of weeks after the film wrapped, the bill finally arrived. To my delight, it was only $1,147. Gulp! My heart stopped and I had to keep repeating to myself that I did not have to pay for it. Sadly, the phone's tab was frighteningly close to my entire salary for this film.

I called the accountant declaring my need for money. He cheerily greeted me with, "Oh, didn't you hear? The film just ran out of money." WHAT!!!!!

I asked the accountant to clarify this for me.

"Do I need to spell it out for you? We can't pay you back because we've got no money left." His voice was shaky with the knowledge that he too could not get his weekly salary until some cash showed up in the bank.

I had no idea what I was going to do. I had no sort of rapport with the producer to just call him up and tell him how badly I needed this money. I decided now was a good time to start that relationship. But like all good fly-by-night producers, he was impossible to reach.

It took me some time, and a few good detective books, but I finally hunted him down and got a hold of his secretary.

I explained the urgency of my monetary problem to his secretary who cared more about the shape of her fingernails than my sad attempt to retrieve my money. All she could say was, "Get in line, honey."

No way, Jose! I was not about to stand for this. I had rent to pay, food to buy, car payments to make. I could NOT afford this outrageous cost.

I had ten days to pay the phone bill or accrue late charges. I did not even want to think about how expensive *that* could get. The secretary droned on about taking my name and number and how someone would get back to me as soon as possible. I could hear the nail filer scrape back and forth.

Days went by and still no word from the producer. Surely he wouldn't let me blow in the breeze like this. I kept calling, faxing, leaving voice and e-mail messages. Nothing was getting this man to respond.

A few days later, the accountant called and asked if I would stop harassing the producer. WHAT?! He thought I was harassing **him**?

The accountant's only response was that they would try to get me my money as soon as they got some of their deposits back from other vendors. I was tiring quickly of this entire matter. I barely had enough in my bank account to buy dinner that night while this arty farty, very well to do, Hancock Park home-owning producer who drove a Rolls Royce thought I was harassing him.

That was all I could take. I called his office and announced in a candy-coated, concerned voice that I needed to talk to the producer immediately. The secretary asked who I was. I replied, "The AIDS clinic. I have some…news for him." I was passed on to him immediately.

The next day I had a check for the full amount rushed over to my apartment via messenger.

CHAPTER SIX

Production Managers—Can't Live with Them, Can't Shoot Them

Production Managers. Ask any random crew member to describe what a production manager does and you'll probably get a blank stare. That's because no one on a set, besides the production managers themselves, knows what they do except yell at people all day long.

Production managers are…interesting. They have the least glamorous above-the-line title mainly because no one aspires to be one of them. Come on, when was the last time you heard a kid say, "When I grow up, I want to be a production manager." It's never going to happen. That's because PMs do all the uncool stuff. They're the ones who battle over salaries and make enemies with the crew when it comes to cutting budgets. They're the ones who have to wipe the producers' butts. They are the ones serving lunch when the caterer up and quits. They are the ones always running around in a quandary with a big fat notebook in hand looking for someone.

But what in the world does this have to do with production assistants? Everything. These are the people a PA should fear most on the set. Production managers are the people who have the ability to make a PA's life a living hell. Forget the producers, directors, or even the actors—they're pussycats in comparison to the wrath of the production manager.

Because production managers are so overwhelmed by an inordinate amount of work, they usually end up going insane. And guess who they take with them.

The Weird, Wild, and Wacko

I was working on an independent film that had gone loopy. We were pulling down eighteen to twenty hour days, six days a week. We were all dragging our toes with exhaustion, but we all stuck with the project because we really believed in it—plus, none of us had any better offers.

Because I was the head office PA, Tony the production manager was always in my face for something. He was a fifty-year-old, stoned face man who took everything so seriously. It got to the point where no one enjoyed being around him because he was always angry.

We were two months into the grueling schedule and we were starting to forget our own names. It's funny what sleep deprivation can do to a group of people. It's not a pretty sight. Everyone looks pale, they either lose or gain a bunch of weight, and they always smell bad because there's no time to bathe regularly.

Tony took it a step further. He would stay at the office all night and crash out on the smelly sofa. Then he'd wake up when the crew arrived in the morning, as if there was nothing odd about him sleeping under newspaper, and he'd go on with his day. We couldn't pass up the opportunity to tease him about his rumpled appearance, but he didn't care.

Days would pass where he'd be wearing the same ratty flannel and jeans ensemble. I don't even think he took the time to take his shoes off when he slept. He certainly didn't comb his hair, and we're pretty sure he never changed his underwear, though no one wanted to pursue that issue with him. And yet, while the rest of us were whining about the long hours and how tired we were, Tony never complained once about anything, even when his beard started growing into his mouth.

It was Monday morning. We were ready to face the remaining five weeks of the shoot all bright eyed and bushy tailed after our whole eighteen-hour weekend. Everything appeared normal in the office. We all went to our stations and did our same old stuff. Except Tony. He was acting weird—okay, weirder than normal.

Still dressed in the same filthy jeans he'd worn for three weeks straight, Tony sat in the corner watching all of us. He said nothing; he just kept shifting his attention to each person in the room. Everyone could feel his eyes burning a hole in them. It was eerie.

Later that day, out of nowhere, he started giggling. This former librarian was not a giggler by nature. Nor did he usually find humor in **anything**. He was always too busy telling us what bad jobs we were doing. So, needless to say, his laughter caught us by surprise. We chalked it up to the mysteries of human behavior on a movie set and went on with our business.

In the days to follow, Tony started acting even more peculiar. He drew strange stick pictures of us falling off cliffs and taped them to our computers without any explanation. We weren't sure whether we should thank him for the odd caricatures or call in a psychiatrist.

Then one day, Tony started to weep uncontrollably for hours. It turned out that his dog had run away from home. We tried to comfort him but it was strange to see this normally stern man babbling incoherently about his pooch named Wally.

When the dog returned home a day later, we thought things would go back to normal. Not a chance. He had gone overboard and there wasn't a lifeboat big enough to save him.

The next Saturday morning around 3 a.m., my phone startled me out of bed. It was Tony. His garbled voice uttered, "Come on, Tiffany. Where are you? You've got to help me."

I begged for him to explain what was wrong and where he was. I was making so much noise that my roommate came into my room scared.

He continued, "Tiffany! Come down here right now. Help me move these trucks."

Trucks?! What trucks?

He kept babbling, "Get your lazy butt out of bed and come help me move our trucks off of Ventura Boulevard. They aren't safe there."

It was twenty-seven hours before I was due at work and this lunatic was talking about trucks that we didn't even have for our film. I was angry. My roommate was angry. Tony's wife was furious.

"Tony," I could hear her yelling, "go back to sleep!"

She pulled the phone away from her zombie husband and said sweetly to me, "I'm so sorry. This film has pushed him over the edge. I'm either going to commit him or divorce him if this movie isn't finished soon."

I asked if he was going to be calling again. She assured me that she would disconnect the phone and hide it. After that she'd be strapping his arms and legs down.

The Nutty Fruit Stand

In my work experience, random acts of insanity are actually common place. On a medium-budget art house flick, I had the opportunity to meet a fine production manager named Monica. Alright, she was gross in every way. First, she was a scraggly woman whose wardrobe consisted of three pastel sweatshirts with faded cats on the front. She constantly talked with her mouth full and thought nothing of hawking a loogy while holding a conversation. If that wasn't enough to make a person vomit, she had a rat's nest for hair that was so greasy. You could lose pens and small animals in there.

She never spoke to anyone except if she was angry with the person. And let me tell you, *anything* could set her off. It could have been that the sour cream was too sour or not creamy enough. It could have been that a name was spelled incorrectly on a phone message. It could have been that someone looked at her funny. Or worse, it could have been that she was mad at her boyfriend. Whoops, she didn't have a boyfriend. And **that** made her really mad!

Around ten o'clock one night, Monica ate a buffalo wing from the craft service table. She spit out the wing declaring that its putrid barbecue sauce sucked.

Rhonda, the seventy-year-old craft service lady with tattoos decorating her neck, was none too pleased about anyone talking badly about her home cooking. She had a sharp tongue and twenty years experience in this business. She was a tough old grandma who didn't take crap from anybody. No one on the crew ever dared to mess with her no matter how horrendous her bean dishes were. Rumor had it that she once killed a snotty director and served him to the crew with a side of Ranch dressing.

Yet, this wasn't enough to keep Monica's mouth shut. No one ever called Monica a smart woman. In fact, Rhonda outwardly called her a &%@!*#, #@!)* moron.

"Oh yeah?" Monica taunted. "If I say your food sucks, then it does!" This was drawing a large crowd. A few of us PAs grabbed whatever food we could and watched the battle. We knew what was coming.

With a blink of a long, fake eyelash, Rhonda took off her apron and packed up her food so fast, Monica didn't know what to say, except, "Uh, um, sorry? Please don't go."

Honestly, like the rest of us, Rhonda was looking for an excuse to jump ship ages ago. She couldn't have been happier to leave, but not without making Monica's life as hellish as she had made hers.

There was no looking back for Rhonda. She had another gig slinging popcorn and chocolate lined up within three minutes of telling Monica where she could shove her yogurt-covered pretzels.

After Rhonda made her grand exit taking anything edible in sight with her, Monica turned fiery red. Smoke started blowing from her ears.

On-lookers quickly dispersed. I looked around and realized I was the only PA still sitting there.

Monica shot me a look and yelled, "Hey!" as I tried to make a break. "Get over here and cut apples."

Apples? Where was she going to find apples? She told me to wait there as she ran outside. Sure enough, she returned with an armful of tiny, deformed apples from the sickly tree in the parking lot.

She handed me a plastic knife and together, in an uneasy silence, we cut half-ripened apples.

It's true that there is some unspoken movie rule saying there needs to be food around at all times. And yes, it's true that the rule doesn't specify that the food has to be particularly tasty, but I don't think anyone was really interested in eating worm-filled apples at that late hour. After all, there was only about an hour to go before we wrapped. But, Monica insisted I cut faster.

Over the walkie-talkie, I heard the assistant director calling me onto the set to deal with some crisis. I explained to Monica that I had to leave our exciting apple-cutting session. She started to cry. I tried to console her but she wildly began throwing apple wedges at the wall.

As I scooted away, I could hear her muttering to the faded cat on her chest, "I can do this, damn it. I think I can. I think I can."

Dr. Jekyll & Ms. Hyde

My friend Lisa was the production manager of a short film that was shooting on weekends. She begged me to be her PA even though she wasn't able to pay me a cent. I told her it would be my pleasure to work with her. I'd do anything to help a friend, even if it did mean working seven days a week. She thanked me profusely for helping her out of a pinch and reassured me that everyone on the show was really cool and fun.

When I got to the set, my friend of two years had turned into a completely different person than I knew. What had they done with my sweet

Lisa? It appeared she had turned into a self-absorbed production manager who insisted on showing her newfound authority.

After we wrapped a sixteen hour shooting day, Lisa told me to take the exposed film to the processing lab. I was tired but I knew she really needed my help.

I didn't know how to get to the lab from the desolate stage that was located in the middle of nowhere. Since she was my friend and all, she offered to lead me close enough to a main street where I'd be able to find my own way. I followed her, thinking to myself, 'Man, what a great friend I have.' I immediately forgave her for being such a pain earlier.

When we got to Santa Monica Boulevard I knew where I was going. Then I realized why I knew where I was going. This was the route to Lisa's house. As a matter of fact, Lisa only lived three blocks from the processing lab. Apparently she was too good to do such a menial task that consisted of (I'm not lying) putting the car in park, carrying two small cans of film inside the lab, placing the cans on a counter, getting back into the car and driving away.

I was fuming because I did not live a mere three blocks from the processing lab. I lived thirty miles away in the complete opposite direction I had just come from.

Concerned about her unusually rude behavior, I called her to resolve things. I called a few times, in fact…and hung up. I then posted her number on a variety of seedy men's restroom walls.

I felt better right away.

CHAPTER SEVEN

Stupid Bosses

It is a certainty in this business that every production assistant will get stuck with idiotic bosses along the career path. It's just as reliable as a baby soiling its diapers. But instead of fighting it, let the crap fall where it may—and then try to find the humor in it all.

Hollywood likes to promote from within the confines of its little inbred circle of disillusioned prodigies. These people would be laughed at in the social structure of real life.

But these industry people are not part of the real world anymore. Their identities, rational emotions, and sensible morals have been stripped away and replaced with greed and the need for power and success at any cost. Or, another way of putting it is—the more money they make, the more work we production assistants have to do. It's all part of the rite of passage into the Hollywood food chain and we must accept it.

However, we production assistants can always laugh about our bosses' stupidity behind their backs and write a book about them.

The Whole Lot of Them

People in Hollywood with any sort of authority (basically anyone who's not a PA) seem to easily confuse perspective. As soon as they have someone to boss around, they seem to abuse their privileges. What am I getting at? Parking lots. Yeah, that's right.

I was a meek little PA happy to play the yes-woman to the location manager of a mini-budget, no named film that never went anywhere. His name was Al. I thought he was a film god because he had worked on a bunch of cool movies. Okay, I admit my reasoning for worshipping him wasn't *that* great.

Al snatched me out of the assistant director's department and showed me the world of locations. I thought I was in heaven. I had my very own cushy chair in our private little location office. We were still working on getting me a desk, but I was happy with the TV dinner tray.

Before I came on board, Al had one of the hardest one-man shows going on in Hollywood. He had no one to support him. He had been working round the clock for five consecutive weeks finding locations at break-neck speeds only to have them rejected left and right by the director and producer. I admired his talent, dedication, and unselfish teamwork as he let me take on more and more of his tasks. We had a great relationship—I thought he was great and he liked me thinking he was great. I wanted to learn everything I could from him.

He saw my eagerness as such a terrific asset to our micro-department. So much so that he decided to put it to good use by loading me up with more and more of his tasks. He felt it was important that I learned through experience. Before I knew it, I was doing everything for him while he was playing games on his computer.

On the eve of our first location shoot-day, Al knocked off early to catch dinner with his friends. I thought that was a little pompous but he obviously was ready for our first day on location with our 50-plus crew in downtown Los Angeles. So, off he ran to play with his friends. I decided to go home and sleep before our early morning call.

Just as I slung my bag across my shoulder, the phone rang. It was Al. He must have been a block away calling on his cherished cellular phone.

"I forgot something," he admitted. I dropped my bag to the floor. Why did I answer the phone?

He told me to go downtown to our site's parking lot because he forgot to cone off our designated parking spots.

"WHAT?!" I screamed into the phone, only it sounded more like, "Okay." And so I went, kicking myself all the way downtown for not being assertive.

It was 10 p.m. I was all by myself carrying seven very heavy orange street cones in the darkened lot. I was instantly greeted by several homeless people who thought I was an ATM. I swung the heavy cones around like a propeller. Wondering which hospital I escaped from, they kept their distance.

I surveyed the lot for a good long time. Frankly, I had no idea which spots were ours to park the crew. I ran to a pay phone and paged Al twelve times. I stood there like an open target on the sidewalk expecting to be accosted by bullets as drugged out bums and prostitutes whistled at me. This wasn't how I wanted to die.

After an eternity, Al finally had the courtesy of calling me back. He explained where he wanted the cones and where I shouldn't forget to block off, and blah, blah, blah. He might as well have been talking Swahili.

While Al blabbered away, I nervously watched a gang of men watching me. I told Al that I understood everything and that he should go back to his guests.

I freaked as the gang came closer towards me so I threw the cones across the entrance of the entire lot.

The band of hoodlums started to hoot and holler at me. I bolted faster than a lawyer could lie.

The next morning Al showed up an hour late to the set because he had had "a hard night." It was all on me to park the crew in our "designated spaces," direct the trucks into place, and have the building opened up. This was why Al was getting paid four times more than I was? And he was sleeping off a hangover? I instantly lost the high admiration I had for him. Oh well, at least I had a date that night with Jimmy, the shoe shining homeless guy.

At the Car Wash

The Cheapness Syndrome is very contagious in Hollywood. The very worst offenders are usually those who make nearly eighty-seven percent of the film's budget.

Rob, a PA on a tremendously generous budgeted film, was working for Betty, one of the most lucrative female producers in the business. Together with her director hubby, they were easily pulling down millions of dollars—*per quarter*. Betty asked Rob to get her Mercedes washed and detailed at her favorite nearby car wash. She handed him a hundred dollar bill…and a finely crumpled three dollar coupon from a car wash in Washington State.

"They accept coupons from their competition. See if that works," she urged.

Rob pulled Betty's brand new, top of the line Mercedes up to the Burbank car wash and presented the tattered coupon. To his embarrassment, the attendant laughed and said, "I'm not accepting that poor excuse of a coupon. That thing expired five years ago."

Rob tried to joke it off by saying, "She must've given me the wrong one."

When Rob brought the expiration date to Betty's attention, she laughed and apologized. However, instead of throwing it away, she tucked that coupon back into her leather Coach wallet with the intention of using it someday, somewhere else. She was a die-hard cheap ass!

Beans, Beans the Magic Fruit…

Nicole liked her job as a PA on a long-running TV sitcom. Or at least, she liked it most of the time. Actually she dreaded the religious lunch hour when all the executives, who made four hundred times her salary, got their meals for free. The production assistants rotated the catering duties so no single person could monopolize all the fun.

When it was Nicole's turn that day, she went around to the seventeen head honchos, writers, and producers. The starving production assistants were not allowed to get anything for themselves on the company's dime. Yet, most of these excessively spoiled rich executives were getting enough food to take home to their families for dinner.

On this particular day, everyone decided they'd be eating from the Mexican joint down the street. Nicole diligently placed the orders carefully checking and rechecking each one over the phone. In fact, she spent twenty minutes on the phone with the restaurant having three different people confirm the order. There was no room for error. Nicole had heard horror stories of what happened to PAs when the lunches weren't right. She vowed never to have that happen to her.

When she got to the restaurant, she and two waiters painstakingly went through all the orders to make sure they were correct. Okay, she sighed with relief, she was ready to face the hungry sharks back at the office.

She laid out the food for the feeding frenzy. She passed out what she could before the piranhas grabbed the rest from her hands. After that group was satisfied with what they got, Nicole took the final orders to the remaining four producers in their offices.

After everyone was served, the only sounds heard were satisfied snorts, grunts, slurps, and paper rattling.

Exhausted, but thoroughly relieved, Nicole went to the refrigerator to scrounge around for some stale bagel remnants for her own little lunch. Suddenly, from behind the associate producer's office door came that oh-too-familiar growl that is not physically possible for a normal female human. A gorilla, maybe.

The boss exclaimed, "Nicole, get your [you can read between the lines] in here! NOW!"

Everyone in hearing distance (the entire city of Burbank) dropped his or her lunch wondering if that was what a seismic boom felt like.

Nicole dropped her soda and looked at the sympathetic eyes of the other two production assistants. They were glad it wasn't them. Nicole gulped and wobbled weakly to the woman's office.

The associate producer yelled, "Nicole, can't you do anything right?! I asked for *%$#@! black beans, not &%#$??@ pinto beans. Black beans are black, pinto beans are brown. Black, brown. Two different colors, two different beans. If I had wanted pinto beans I would have asked for pinto beans. Do you understand?!"

Swallowing her humiliation, Nicole offered to go back to the restaurant and resolve the problem.

The associate producer balked insistently, "But then my tostado will get cold." Then, as though Nicole was a gnat, the boss-devil rudely waved her out of the office.

A half hour later, as lunch was winding down, poor Nicole's stomach was tied in knots. She could not eat because she felt so hurt. The associate producer stormed out of her office and threw her untouched tostado and pinto beans in the wastebasket right next to Nicole's desk.

Nicole looked longingly at the wasted food but the thought of snatching it out of the wastebasket made her ill. It wasn't because of germs, it was because she could not stand the idea of eating anything that her flagitious boss' fingers had touched.

Instead, Nicole went back to picking at her stale bagel pieces and sticking pins in her voodoo doll.

Happy Birthday to Me

It was my first birthday away from home. I was feeling lonely, but I had to go to work and make my embarrassingly inept salary as an illustrious production company's PA. As much as I wanted to spend my day of birth with those who made it possible, I knew I had to work my butt off every day to gain the respect of these prestigious film people. Telling them I wanted to go home to Mommy wasn't going to let me earn that.

When I realized I wasn't going home, I lifted my head high and dropped the most obvious hints around the office that my birthday was coming up soon. I even wrote it on the office calendar in neon pink with electronically blinking arrows.

My co-workers saw it and asked, "Oh, it's your birthday this Thursday?"

Yes, this was working!

However, when the big commemorative day of my origin came, everyone seemed to go brain dead. After all those hints I had dropped, all those flowers I had sent myself, and all those pretend phone calls I had made loudly stating the importance of that day, it turned out I was sharing a birthday with the producer of the company.

Great, how was I supposed to compete with *him* when celebrities like Sly, Sharon, and Julia were calling to wish *him* well? The kitchen was full of presents and cakes that were sent to *him* from every Hollywood big-wig imaginable.

My boss ran over to me frantically with an order slip in her hand. "Go to this bakery and pick up the cake…" (For me? Ahhh, how sweet.) "…for the producer."

When I finally got my message across about what a funny coincidence it was that little ol' me shared the same glorious day of nativity as the producer, it was like a sack of bricks fell on my boss.

She looked at me blankly and droned, "Oh, I had no idea. Could you light the candles on the producer's cake?"

What?! Weren't my banners or the skywriting enough of a clue? Yes it was *my* birthday!

Fortunately, it was only around noon when I made it perfectly clear to the entire office that I was entitled to being celebrated as well. I figured they had their lunch break to go pick out a nice gift…or a goofy card…or even some scurvy flowers outside.

Yet, by five o'clock that evening, I got nothing more than a dry: "Oh yeah, happy birthday" from a few people who cared more about what was in their noses than they did about me. Besides, everyone was too busy whooping it up with the producer who was conducting drinking games in his office.

I could have taken the day off and forfeited my pitiful daily wage to fly home where my family was actually celebrating my birthday for me. I got a call at work from my loving family who was eating a nice dinner to commemorate my existence.

I wanted to cry. I wanted to scream. I wanted someone in that office to care half as much for me as they did about the producer who was, at that point, sprawled across his desk as the secretaries sprayed whip cream all over him.

Just as I was about to hop on the next plane home, the temp secretary (who had been there only two days) convinced my boss to get me a cake.

I was so happy that this new woman cared that much about me. She was obviously the ONLY one! It didn't matter. I had no desire to hold any grudges, especially since they were finally going to celebrate me for once. Minutes later I was called into my boss' office. I was so eager for some big surprise.

I got a surprise all right. My boss handed me twenty bucks and told me to go pick up my own cake at the bakery. Then she asked if I could swing by the office supply store. They were low on paper clips.

Loony Tunes

Normally production accountants have little to do with the production assistant except when they need us to deliver a check or something. On a small budget film, I had the pleasure of working with the accountant from hell. For some reason she thought of herself more like the producer. She was always bossing people around, even the producer himself.

Her name was Angelica and let me tell you, there was nothing angelic about her. She basically had zilch going for her—not a whit of a brain and no personality except for a vicious, foaming bark. She was so dumb she couldn't even write checks correctly. And what a temper she had. We're talking Leona Helmsley meets Godzilla on a bad hair day. She'd start yelling at people as soon as she walked in the door. One day she came to work late and yelled at all of us for being on time and making her look bad.

The question on everyone's mind was how could this wacko be allowed to work on this show with an attitude like that?

The answer came straight from the production manager's mouth when he said, "We're afraid to fire her."

The producers tried to fire her once but she threatened to hit them with a lawsuit running the gamut of racial to sexual to hairstyle discrimination.

We production assistants were downright horrified to be in the same room as her, especially when she was having a hard time figuring out the books. During pre-production, balancing the books had become so overwhelming for her that she would spend nights at the office.

After a week straight of all-nighters, she demanded some help. We all demanded she get some help, but we were thinking something *different*.

The producers and the production manager deliberated behind closed doors for an hour before they came up with a solution that fell short of getting this woman a straight jacket. They offered her a sacrificial production assistant to help ease the workload—you know, someone who actually *knew* how to add and subtract.

To fairly settle who would risk life and limb for such a glamorous position, we played Ro-Sham-Bo. Out of the three of us PAs, Walt was the one thrown to the wolf.

That evening, Walt sat uncomfortably by Angelica's side trying to hide his nervous shivering. All along, he waited with nauseated anxiety for her to pile on the work. Time and time again, throughout the long evening, she would delegate a job over to Walt. Then she'd change her mind figuring it would be faster to do it herself rather than wasting time explaining how it was supposed to be done. The problem simply was she couldn't explain something that she didn't know how to do.

It was midnight and everyone had gone home except for Walt and Dragon Lady. Still, she had given Walt nothing to do, yet she would not allow him to go home. Until 4 a.m., Walt watched her watch the computer screen and not touch a single button except to remove the screen saver every few minutes. If Walt made a sound, even to clear his throat, she would give him the evil eye. He was even too afraid to go to the bathroom.

This lasted four days straight. Walt was not getting home until three or four in the morning only to return three hours later to start it again. He was going insane.

At last, he went to the producers and gave them the ultimate ultimatum. It was either Angelica or him.

The producers and the production manager deliberated behind closed doors for an hour before announcing their decision. Justice prevailed…Walt was fired.

This is of course was what Walt wanted because he could then go on unemployment before he was hired a month later on a gargantuan budget studio flick.

That left us two remaining PAs vulnerable to Angelica. However, just as we were forced to play a round of thumb war to determine our fate, Angelica decided she was changing careers. The next day she moved to Las Vegas to deal Black Jack.

Mother's Milk

Laura was the office PA of a long running television series. It was a great show, but like any of them, it had its share of outrageously demanding Hollywood types. Mary, the assistant director, was one of those lovely people who always kept the production assistants on their feet.

Laura was busy filing and answering phones one day when Mary frantically called from the nearby stage exclaiming, "Laura, I was just paged by KinderCare. Little Sammy's ready for his feeding and I can't leave the set. The poor little boopie-whoop is crying. My God, Laura, you should have heard my precious son's screams for help!"

Mary had whipped herself into a maniacal frenzy. "You know how hard it is to leave your two month old in the care of strangers?" She was now yelling into the phone. "It's tough, I tell you!" She was choking up between sobs.

Laura was more interested in what this cry-fest was leading up to and what she was going to have to do about it. Sure, Mary was a decent person despite her lunatic ways of claiming EVERYTHING was an emergency, but that was not Laura's main concern here. The bottom line was—Laura wasn't about to nurse that kid on her own breast.

Mary continued to ramble and finally screamed for her to come to the set because this was "an emergency."

On the set, Laura found Mary in a dressing room cowering in a corner. She rushed to help Mary who looked like she was doubled over in pain. Laura moved in to find Mary pumping breast milk. Laura almost passed out from the whole naturalness of the sight.

Mary saw the green look on Laura's face and said, "I hate to ask you, but could you help me here?"

Laura wasn't too keen on this idea. Sure childbirth, motherhood, and all that crap were blessings. But come on, she did not feel the need to know her boss **this** well.

Mary broke down into tears wailing, "Come on. For the love of Sammy, this is an emergency. Pump, damn it. Pump!"

After about an eternity of Laura pumping this awkward contraption, trying to look as far away from Mary as possible, Mary finally let out a sigh of relief.

"It's filled. Boy, I feel like a cow," she laughed...by herself. Laura couldn't get to the door fast enough before Mary chimed in, "Now take this to the KinderCare. And hurry. It's an emergency." Same old Mary, naked and all.

Laura was off and running, holding the bottle as if it were a live fish. She gently laid the bottle upright in the passenger seat strapping it in with the seat belt. In a split second, she gunned the engine and was peeling down Olive Street. The sense of urgency wasn't so much about Sammy as it was to simply get away from Mary's boobs.

Perhaps she was much too prissy about all this, Laura thought to herself. Perhaps she should consider working with a therapist on her maladjusted insecurities, she thought as she rounded a corner. The bottle hurled against the window before slamming against the dashboard and landing back onto the seat.

Laura looked over in alarm at the bottle that was trickling breast milk onto her leather upholstery. Ahhh! She did not care *how* weird her insecurities were, this was downright disgusting. She pulled the car over and ripped her trunk open for some sort of quick solution.

Voila! The emergency kit. And was this ever an emergency!

She yanked the kit open and went to work. When she was finished, the broken bottle was wrapped in gauze and bandages and was still three-fourths full of the precious milk. Good ol' Sammy couldn't have been happier.

Hello?...

It was about 10:30 a.m. All of us underling PAs had been at the office since 7:30 a.m. per the boss' strict instructions. We were working our butts off trying to keep an orderly office without our key leader's presence. Where the hell was she? As great as it was to have her absence, we were incapable of managing the office properly without her. People were calling with questions we could not answer and problems we could not solve. Our location department was starting to look inept. As much as I hated to admit it, our boss was an important source of knowledge needed to run the office.

But no one had heard from her since the previous evening. She hadn't answered any of her pages. Finally, she called in on her cellular phone and told us she was downtown all that time at a very important meeting with the city officials. She said she was in the middle of trying to get us a tricky permit for our shoot. She told us to page her if we needed her.

While a couple of us were excited to know that we had some more time to goof off, one of the more skeptical PAs didn't buy her story. He picked up the phone and called her house. Stupidly enough, she answered. She had never been downtown that whole morning. Instead, she was working out on her treadmill with the television blaring.

Please learn from my boss' mistake. If you say you're somewhere work-related but you are really goofing off at home, DO NOT answer your phone. That's why God invented answering machines!

CHAPTER EIGHT

How to Deal with Stupid Bosses

Retribution is always a good thing in circumstances where your boss is a total idiot and thinks you are his or her slave. Personally, I'm always on the side of the PA who has been served great injustice. I don't care how big or how petty. Keep in mind that you, the production assistant, are never wrong about hating your boss. It's all part of the game. Having said that, I now give you my ways of dealing with stupid bosses. (I'm not bitter, I swear!)

You Talk Too Much...

The cellular phone is one of the most easily inconspicuous ways to trick your boss. Here's the scenario: Let's say the boss calls you at the office from the road on the cellular phone. Ninety percent of the time the bosses in Hollywood are en route to the office and have nothing to say that couldn't wait another fifteen minutes. They just like to rub their company-expensed cellular privileges in our faces. If the conversation is wasting your time, there are a couple of ways to eliminate it all together.

First, rattle into your receiver to fake a bad connection. Paper works pretty well but some prefer aluminum foil for a more advanced mechanical failure sound. Speak into the receiver, "Hello? Boss, are you still there? Hello? I can't hear—"

Then hang up.

If you can't find a rattling tool nearby, it's acceptable to simply say you can't hear them and hang up. If your boss is truly worried about the cellular phone not working, he or she may have you running all over town to fix the problem. Of course, this could be a good thing because then you'll have more free time to waste. (See next story.)

Scenario number two: You're tired of senselessly driving around town polluting the air and wasting your gas on errands that are not serving the welfare of the film or television project. You've decided you want to stop the frivolous runs to the producer's favorite Beverly Hills salon or the cigar shop in Malibu.

How do you go about doing this without getting fired? You come out and tell them you're having car trouble. The best line I have found is: "My brakes are failing. I hope I can make it home alive tonight but sure I'll be happy to run that errand for you. I'm covered under your insurance policy, right?"

Or another good "excuse" is: "My car's in the shop and I had to be driven to work. I'll take your brand new, fully loaded sport utility vehicle if you'd like." Then watch the expression on your boss' face.

Perhaps flat out lying isn't your style. No problem. Simply put a fake cast on your right foot. When anyone asks what happened, just shake your head and say you'd rather not talk about it. Make sure the cast is clunky enough so it could never fit on the gas pedal. Why stop there? Put a cast anywhere on your body and you're guaranteed a nice cushy chair by the phone and fax machine.

Scenario number three: You've just plain had it and can't bear to face the rest of the day at work. You could always fake a good case of dysentery or a temporary loss of hearing, but personally I think you're more likely to get sympathy with what ails your boss. Announce calmly that the voices in your head are telling you to see your therapist this instant.

Exclaim wildly that your Prozac prescription is **finally** ready and beg if you can be excused to go pick it up. If they protest, gently let them know what you're like without your medication.

"Go pick up..."

I love when a boss starts a sentence like "Go pick up..." Inevitably it means you, the PA *with a car,* are going to be on your own, out of sight from any supervisors for a little while. The farther away and more seemingly complex the errand, the better because it gives you, the PA *with a car,* more time to fool around.

The people sending PAs out on assignments generally have no concept of how long they really take to complete. My advice is to milk it for all the time you can. Even if someone ever **did** confront you for taking too long—the old 'traffic was murder' excuse works every time. Come on, this is Los Angeles, home of the smog, plastic surgery, and gazillions of miles of jammed freeways that we're talking about here!

If you are ever stuck in a creative pinch and can't think of anything to do with your "free time," here are some of my personal favorites:

Get your hair cut.

Get your oil changed.

Do your banking. There's always a paycheck to deposit or an ATM to pillage. Order new checks or open a new account. Stand in line over and over again.

Grocery shop for yourself. Do not buy anything that will spoil, unless you can come home for some well deserved R&R.

Get your car washed. You may even be able to expense it with petty cash if you do it right.

Go home and take a nap or catch up on your television viewing. Always be aware of the time or else this could get risky. And never **ever** answer your phone while ditching work!

Go to the pet store and make friends with some cute kittens and puppies.

Buy yourself some new clothes.

Write that screenplay that's going to break you out of this PA spot and put you on top of the Hollywood food chain.

Workout. This can make you look extremely hard working when you come back to work all sweaty.

Take a long lunch break.

Grab a beer or three.

Go to an Alcoholics Anonymous meeting and make some good business contacts.

Make friends with the unemployed film people or fellow ditching PAs at the local coffee shops.

Go to the beach and learn how to surf. Don't get your pager wet!

Take in a movie. However, expect the production coordinator to page you during the best scene.

Test-drive new cars. See if you look better in a Porsche or Ferrari for when you're rich and famous.

Then of course do not forget to actually complete the mission you were sent out to do. Also remember to benefit from the errand. No, I don't mean in an educational manner. If you're picking up office supplies, get a few binders, envelopes, or a nice recliner for yourself. It's only right.

Don't worry or feel bad about it because when you're a big time producer or CEO of a studio, your production assistants will steal from you, too.

Fun With Petty Cash

Now if you are lucky enough to receive a stash of petty cash, then you can have the same kind of fun as cheap bosses do all over the industry. Here are a few suggestions for what you can do with the money for your own pleasure.

Buy lottery tickets. A fellow PA made it a weekly habit to buy five tickets every morning with the bagels. One time, she won seventy-five bucks!

Buy a lifetime of vitamins. Every office in Los Angeles can appreciate being healthy. I can't even fathom how many times I have been sent to health food stores and gourmet grocery stores to stockpile the offices' kitchens with Echinacea and colon cleansers. When they send you, don't forget yourself…each and every time. Just repeat after me: "I'm worth it!"

Buy groceries. Always put a few of your favorite items on the company shopping list.

Buy art and office supplies. These are receipts that are easily hidden when slipped in with the rest of your receipts. Do I really need to repeat this? If you work in a production office, they need these things anyway. How are the accountants to know that they never received two extra boxes of staples and a couple of rulers? Remember, these make great gifts for friends and family members.

Buy stamps. Then write to all of your friends on the company's impressive letterhead about how you were promoted to producer.

Buy party supplies. I know PAs who threw grand parties all thanks to petty cash. They bought everything from the chips to the decorations to the kegs of beer—all courtesy of some of the biggest studios in Hollywood. (Note to all law enforcement officials: it wasn't me, I swear.)

Now how do you buy liquor on the company, you ask. There are ways around the system (if you have not figured that out already). First, you can always buy yourself anything at stores like 7-Eleven. Many such convenient stores conveniently give customers unmarked receipts. I've also heard of PAs investing in their own cash registers to create receipts.

Be cautioned to keep these fake receipts to small amounts because they're easier to hide. Anything worth doing right takes a little time. The key is to not raise suspicions. Do not let your boss see you reading this book!

CHAPTER NINE

The Joys of Location Shooting

Shooting on location brings on a whole new level of headaches for production assistants. If you thought directors, actors, and producers were bad, wait until your protective stage walls are stripped away and you are forced to deal with the scariest monsters of all—the public. Hold me.

Love Thy Neighbor— Until They Start Making Noise

Neighbors can be your greatest allies or your absolute enemies when you are filming in their territory. I've known neighbors to bake cookies for film crews because they were so excited to be a part of a real film or commercial.

I've also known neighbors to drive in circles swearing at how we film people should be shot for being such a nuisance to the community.

Then there's another sector of the public made up of reasonable individuals who accept that filming will always be a fact of Southland living. They embrace these pure Los Angeles moments by appreciating the crew's artistic contribution to society. Screw that, these savvy folks just want to exploit these cinematic opportunities for their own financial benefit. And the best way to do that is by being a royal pain in the wazoo!

Some people choose gardening equipment, preferably weed-whackers or gasoline-run leaf blowers, to get noticed. Electric saws also create fabulous disturbances sure to get the director and sound department to pull out their hair. Some of the lazier, less creative folks stick to encouraging their dogs to bark all day or turning music up to blast out the entire city.

Generally, these annoyances will attract a sizable payoff from the production company to keep quiet. The typical scenario goes as follows: the neighbor blasts his noise from his desired source which will instigate an immediate response from the normally friendly locations department.

Someone from the locations department will find the closest PA to make the noise stop. The PA will proceed with a scripted speech that goes something like: "We are in the middle of shooting a very big motion picture with an unhappy actor. Would you please keep the noise down?"

Like this means anything to the neighbor whose eyeballs have been removed and replaced with large dollar signs.

Words of disgust are then spewed from the enraged neighbor who has a problem with this film crew censoring him in the sanctuary of his home. Some of the angrier people will go on to explain how hard they've worked to pay for their homes, how stressful their lives are, and how they don't even like to watch movies because they're too expensive. (Please note: the pity thing works well, especially on PAs like me who are given a lot of $20 bills and are told to start the bidding low in exchange for quiet.)

On a semi-low budget film, I once paid a gentleman eighty dollars a day for three days so he wouldn't blast his Van Halen music. His next door neighbor confided to me that the man was normally very quiet except when film companies came into town.

We could have called the police on this man for disturbing the peace but that would have caused resentment against us and future film companies who wished to use that neighborhood. Alright, alright, the reality was that we didn't *technically* have a permit to shoot there that day. Had the man known that, he could have taken us for a heck of a lot more money.

I often considered retiring from all those rough PA gigs and simply follow film companies around Los Angeles. Just me, a pot, and a mallet. I could have been a millionaire by now.

Just Add Water

While working on a film that was set on a lake, Ellen's job as a PA was to be the boat wrangler. It was her duty to make certain the boat was where it was needed at all times. What made Ellen so qualified for this job, you ask? She was the only one foolish enough to admit she had touched an oar before.

On this particular day, the scene recreating the late 1800's was taking place within the confines of a tiny two-person boat. The actor and actress were squirming inside uncomfortably while the director and the camera crew in the nearby boat framed up the shot. Ellen was standing by in her rowboat with the hair/make-up woman.

Actors are usually irritable and demanding as it is but strand them helplessly in a boat in the middle of a deep lake with an overly passive and indecisive director on a hot day and you are just asking for a disaster.

The thirty-something actor started complaining like an impatient little brat about how long it was taking to set up the shot. He was whining about being hot in his costume and how "overall disenchanted" he was and how "highly rudimentary" this film was. He was British and loved to throw flowery words out like that. The crew was ready to throw him out of the boat.

Then the fussy actress started having her own temper tantrum. Her complaint was that the humidity was making her hair "unfabulously flat."

"I need poof," she pouted.

Ellen had to row the hairdresser over to the actress to ease the hair issues. Ellen carefully eased the rowboat up next to the actors' dingy while the hairdresser reached in to comb the woman's hair. Ellen was having a devil of a time keeping the two boats together while the actress was cautiously leaning into Ellen's boat for the hairdresser to finish her up.

While the actress was being tended to, the actor was getting downright petulant because the sun was in his eyes. He told the director if he didn't get to wear sunglasses in the scene, he was walking off the set. The passive director meekly over-explained how people back in the late 1800's did not even know what sunglasses were…blah, blah, blah.

The actor feigned falling asleep from another stupid story the director was famous for telling. Because of the actor's over-dramatics, the boat started to wobble. This freaked the actress out because she was still leaning into Ellen's boat.

The actress screamed, "Shut it. I'm trying to get pretty."

Impatient with the actor's petty little problem, the actress went back to getting her hair fluffed. The actor continued his war over the sunglasses. He threatened to involve the Actor's Guild if he didn't get his way. Like a weakling, the director tried to deflect this embarrassing confrontation by physically hiding behind the gruff Australian director of photography for security.

The director of photography was never one to beat around the bush. He flat out said to the actor, "You can't wear the stupid glasses, you ass. So knock it off."

This did not sit well with the pompous actor. He stood up abruptly, ready to kill someone, and leaped into the director's boat. By the laws of physics, the actress' off-balanced little dingy turned upside down thoroughly dunking the costumed beauty.

If you've ever seen a cat react to water, you might have **some** idea of this actress' reaction. According to Ellen, it was funny, horrifying, and embarrassing to watch. The actress started screaming at the top of her lungs what an idiot the actor was, though she used slightly different adjectives.

The actor rebutted by telling her what a bad actress she was. Then they both yelled at the director for letting him/her be a part of this production. That's when the director of photography tried to hit both of them with an oar.

The actor and actress immediately quit. Subsequently, their absence shut down the show. The crew had only completed ten and a half days of their thirty-two day shoot and the film as a whole was already about $250,000 into the $350,000 budget. It was a hopeless situation that ended up bankrupting the director who was also the producer.

To Pee or Not to Pee

Camille was an adventurous, sometimes dim-witted, but always lovable PA. She could tell the dirtiest jokes with a sweet, innocent smile on her face. When she found out she'd be working on a comedy film inside a jail, her heart almost stopped from the sick thrill of it all.

Even though she had attended Catholic school in her safe little world of Suburbia—where the most exciting thing to happen was a new window display at The Gap—she was always fascinated by criminals. She was a big fan of "America's Most Wanted."

When she found out that this downtown Los Angeles penitentiary was not open to the criminals yet, she was disappointed. After all, she was hoping to get a date.

It was the crew's first filming day at the prison. Everything was going well except the walkie talkies weren't transmitting inside the heavy-duty steel building. For that reason, the production assistants had to be extra careful to keep the areas quiet.

Camille was assigned to lock down a desolate hallway of jail cells. There she sat alone for hours having no idea whether or not the cameras were rolling. It didn't matter to Camille anyway. She was content imagining burly convicts roaming the hallways in shackles and crooning sad songs of lost freedom as they leaned on the bars.

Actually there were no traditional bars in these cells. Instead, each one had solid steel doors with slit windows. For Camille, it just wasn't the same as her recurring Alcatraz fantasy. But she didn't dwell on the issue. She closed her eyes and went back to her reverie as she sipped her Sprite and tried to remember the words to "Jail House Rock."

Suddenly that all too familiar feeling hit her—she had to pee. She didn't have to pee a little—she had to go so badly that her legs couldn't cross. She didn't know what to do. If she opened that door leading to the set, she could wreck a take. Chances were they weren't shooting at all, but it didn't matter because Camille couldn't even stand up straight let alone be able to get past the crew without leaving a trail of puddles behind.

She rocked back and forth but that was only making her bladder madder. Her eyes were going to roll back into her head if she didn't take control of the situation immediately. She looked the Sprite can over with the thought of squatting over it. No, she thought, her aim was terrible.

She scanned the area for a message to fall from heaven. Then, as if angels were singing to her, her gaze stumbled upon an inviting, shiny steel urinal inside a cell. Her eyes became misty with joy.

She ran inside the cell with her pants around her knees. Just then, she heard a noise and knocked the steel cell door closed for a little privacy.

In complete isolation, Camille relieved herself. This was an epic pee. The kind that goes on for an entire commercial break and then some. The kind of pee that reminds you of Niagara Falls. The kind of pee that makes you sigh with pride.

After she finished her business, she looked up to see what she had done. That's right, she locked herself in jail. She pulled, she pushed, she pounded, she kicked, she screamed, she cried. But no one could hear her throughout that empty hallway.

She started to pace nervously. She mentally went through her stress management therapy and told herself to relax. After all, what was the worst case scenario? SHE COULD DIE AND NO ONE WOULD FIND HER BODY UNTIL THEY THREW SOME UGLY MURDERER IN THERE NAMED SPIKE! But now if Spike was cute...

At the same time, the crew was feasting on a delicious catered lunch with a live steel drum band playing in celebration of the actor's birthday. After the second course, a couple of production assistants started wondering where Camille could be. They realized neither of them had told her it was lunchtime. They dashed over to Camille's assigned hallway but there was no sign of her anywhere.

Inside, Camille was waiting for the Grim Reaper to take her when she heard the other production assistants calling her name. She was saved! Well, the two PAs couldn't exactly swing the prison door open. They had to find the location manager who had to call an officer who had to get the sheriff who had to go to the control tower where he had to find the instructions to open Camille's cell with the control tower's complex computer system.

By the time Camille was released, the whole crew was laughing about her ordeal. The assistant director wisely stationed Camille right outside the building next to an easily accessible public bathroom.

A Job That's for The Birds

A very big budget means a very big star. And every big star needs a signature quirk. One particular comedian's was refusing to loop his dialogue. In other words, you either got this star's hyper-comedic talent on the set the first time or you were stuck with a sound nightmare.

I suppose that, if by the age of thirty-five, you've earned the amount of the United States' trade deficit, you can be as quirky as you want.

There is an old adage in Hollywood—the more money you make, the less work you do. At twenty million dollars a film, this guy could have hired an actor to fill in for him altogether.

As a location PA on this film, I was stuck with the ordeal of keeping our outdoor location quiet for his majesty's comedic perfection to happen without any snags. A few weeks before shooting, I was told to do something about the raucous birds in the trees that lined this posh South Pasadena neighborhood during spring. Sure, why don't I just stop the sun from rising while I'm at it!

Throughout my research, I called every bird expert in the Southland. These wonderful fowl people suggested I do everything from putting fake owls and snakes in the trees to blowing off horns and firecrackers. One gentleman thought it might be a good idea to spray the friendly feathered creatures with a fire hose. Another wise animal lover fancied the idea of putting netting over the entire grove of trees. He explained this would prevent birds from nesting, though unfortunately it would kill the birds that had *already* nested.

I could tell this bird issue was going to get us lots of support from the bird-loving neighborhood.

I submitted lists and lists of suggestions to the producer ranging from absolutely laughable to completely inane. I stood my ground by jumping up and down pulling out my hair screaming, "Tell me you guys are kidding!"

The relentless producer was very serious about finding a solution and scoured my suggestion lists for anything remotely plausible. He came across one that struck him as potentially effective while being harmless to the cute little birdies. Let the record show that he was just as concerned as the rest of us about doing this properly. After all, nuclear warfare was too expensive.

The next day I was sent out to the street to see if the plan he chose would work. Imagine a sweet, non-threatening young woman walking up and down a residential street holding a ridiculously enormous, white helium balloon thirty feet high in the air with great big black eyes painted on it. I called it the Bird Shoo-Awayer™.

Now picture how neighbors in this expensive community viewed my suspicious manner. I was so embarrassed. I was drawing a crowd of on-lookers in the distance. They were arguing over who should call the police on me. I was trying so hard to act like I wasn't doing anything odd. When I turned to them, in an attempt to explain my actions, they scattered into their homes as though I had a toe growing out of my forehead.

I took a moment to pull myself together. I had no reason to let these people get to me. I was violating no laws, plus I was working on a major motion picture. I lifted my head up and proudly set my sights on testing my Bird Shoo-Awayer™.

Of course on that day there were no birds around. While the neighbors peered through their blinds, I had to search the trees for signs of life. Eventually, I found a single blue jay high up in one of the oak trees. From the street, I positioned myself under the bird and slowly raised the beastly balloon predator beside it.

Guess what. Birds are a lot smarter than we humans give them credit for. This bird was not about to budge for a silly balloon. I swear I heard chirps of laughter coming from surrounding trees. I started feeling a little paranoid like this was some sort of twisted remake of Alfred Hitchcock's *The Birds*.

I continued down the street with my black-eyed balloon taunting whatever bird I could find. Not one bird was scared away. That is, not until I put the balloon right underneath a sparrow's butt and watched in delight as it flew away.

Excellent, I thought. My scheme was going according to plan...until the bird landed on a higher branch.

A passing couple smiled at me sympathetically as if to say to each other, "Oh honey, look at the cute mentally challenged girl."

Despite the phenomenal success of my Bird Shoo-Awayer™, I was forced to use some sort of alternative measure. I asked the producer for advice.

He simply stated, "I advise you to make it work." Well thank you, Oh Wise One.

On the day of our shoot, I came armed with a neon pink and green Supersoaker 5000XXZ with two massive water tanks, the most powerful pump legal on a water gun, and a spray in excess of thirty-five feet. When filled, this thing weighed as much as a small cow.

My attempts certainly did not make the birds quiet. These smart feathered friends flew to a branch right above my thirty-five-foot stream and continued their merry chirping. It didn't take me long to realize that if you spray water directly up in the air, that same water will come back down to hit *you*. I wasn't sure who was the bigger idiot here—me or the producer who was still convinced that birds could be quieted.

Super Dog Woman

It was a sweltering Southern California summer afternoon and we were all dead tired from a draining day of a long string of location days. The multi-million dollar actor was irritable and temperamental. He was sweaty and cranky. This made the hair and make-up crew sweaty and crankier. That made the director cranky and mean. In turn, it was causing the producer to become more cranky and meaner than usual. So basically we were just like one big family—mad at each other.

At the same time, we were experiencing some technical difficulties with the camera. This setback was adding to the intense financial pressures that had been building since the beginning of the film. After a lot of perspiration, a lot of cursing, and a little beer, the camera was finally ready to go. The crew was ready. The actor was ready. Places, lights, camera, action.

As if on cue, the entire neighborhood dog population erupted into a grand symphony of barking and howling. This was a classic case of canine conspiracy. One never realizes how many dogs live within a two block radius until one has to stop each and every one of them from barking during a take.

This was a job for only one person—Super Dog Woman. Otherwise known as—me. I was hot, sweaty, and tired with super-sized blisters killing my feet. These minor inconveniences weren't enough to stop *Super Dog Woman*.

I jumped on the ten speed bike provided to me by the props department and set off with my dog biscuit box in hand while the crew cheered me on. It was all on me to quiet each and every dog before any more filming could go on. Talk about pressure!

I biked up to the first house and rang the unsuspecting neighbor's doorbell. I begged the kind owners to keep their sweet pups silent. They gladly complied to help out "a real life major motion picture." This would be a cinch, I thought.

I soon realized that not all the other homeowners were so conveniently home. They were all out making money so they could feed their yappy, demanding dogs. But this wasn't anything to worry about. After all, I was Super Dog Woman capable of quieting down any dog or bird.

The next house was home to two mammoth sized German Shepherds. I looked the growling guard dogs square in the eyes. That only seemed to make them angrier until I talked to them in baby talk and squeezed a few thousand dog biscuits under the gate. I don't care if we're talking about a Rottweiler or a Wiener, no dog can resist my baby voice and delicious dog bones.

Onto the next house I biked. The vicious barks were coming from inside. Each time I knocked on the front door, the two dogs pushed on it. The door bulged with each gale of pooch force. Obviously no one was home. By the sounds of the growls, I think the dogs had eaten their owners.

The door had a mail slot. I opened it slowly to throw in some biscuits. All of a sudden, a dinosaur-sized paw with razor sharp claws swiped the biscuits clean out of my hand. That kept them quiet for the second it took to inhale those miniscule snacks. These monsters needed something more to gnaw on so I tossed a tree branch in the slot.

As I quieted the fifty-seventh dog, I listened to the beautiful sound of neighborhood silence. I was overcome with relief that I didn't even notice the Irish Setters licking my arm from behind a gate. I got on the radio and told the crew that they were safe to proceed. It was all quiet on the western front. The assistant director revered me as a dog queen.

However, these furry intellects weren't about to let me go so fast. You see, the only problem with bribing a dog with food is that *they* suddenly become in control of the situation. These hounds knew they could keep me captive by threatening to bark if they didn't get another pat on the head and another nibble of food.

When the pressure got too tough for only one Super Dog Woman, I initiated some straggling neighborhood kids into my super hero club. These rugrats had been kicked off the film set about two hundred times that day so they were happy to do anything to get close to their actor idol. In return for keeping the dogs hushed, they asked for the actor's autograph. These seven year olds were going to go far in this business. But until then, they were stuck with a forged autographed on a cocktail napkin.

Production Assistants Lost in Space

Dazelle was new to the biz but she knew what it took to become a good production assistant—a spit and venom mentality, the presence of a petunia, and the patience of a sidewalk. That was her—to a T.

When Pamela, the 2nd 2nd assistant director of a high profile comedy film, offered her a PA job, Dazelle jumped on the opportunity faster than a Hollywood call girl could name her price. She was so happy. Her friends were excited. Her parents were proud she was finally putting her engineering degree to some use.

She reported to the Los Angeles Airport for her first day. For two weeks the crew would be shooting all over the airport—from the tarmac to the terminal. Dazelle was taking it all in with an enormous grin from ear to ear. She thanked her lucky stars for this opportunity to become a part of the film community.

Pamela assigned her to the temporary production office where she would answer phones. The makeshift office was set up in an old, abandoned terminal across the tarmac.

Since no one was allowed to simply stroll onto the tarmac where jets were taking off and touching down every two seconds, the only way Dazelle could get out to this tiny, dilapidated building was to be driven out by an airport security officer.

After a ten minute drive from the main terminal, the officer briskly deposited Dazelle at the deserted terminal and sped off. She was all alone inside the dingy, creepy, so-called office that was nothing more than two phones on a folding table. The terminal looked like it was last used in the 1960's for commuter travelers destined for Palm Springs.

The brown vinyl was rotting off the seats. The green wallpaper had long since faded and fallen. The humidity inside was approximately a thousand percent. The floor was the most tolerable piece of furniture in the joint.

Dazelle was bored to death by the isolation. For the entire half hour she stood in a disgusted silence, the phones didn't ring once. There was nothing here to do except pull out crusty foam from the old cushions. There wasn't even a rat or cockroach to keep her company. She counted down the hours until lunch.

She tried to make radio contact with Pamela back at the main terminal to let her know her presence here was pointless. But she couldn't send or receive any signal because they were too far away. If the phones were to ring, she was incapable of getting a message to anyone. She didn't even know anyone's cell phone number.

At the same time, the rest of the crew was comfortably enjoying the air-conditioned terminal near the all-important craft service table. The scene they were shooting was fun. Everyone was having a ball.

Back at the morgue, Dazelle waited, hoping someone would bring her from the set to the lunch tent. No such luck. Lunchtime came and went, and no one remembered her. She started gnawing on the crusty cushion foam.

After about eight hours into the twelve-hour day, she finally wised up that no one cared about her. A bright smile illuminated her face as she decided to give herself the rest of the afternoon off. See if they noticed her then, she thought.

The next morning, Dazelle arrived ready to explain herself to Pamela. It turned out that Pamela quit only hours after sending Dazelle to hell. On top of that, Pamela neglected to tell anyone she had hired Dazelle, let alone assigned her to the worthless task in no man's land.

The next day, Dazelle stationed herself in front of the craft service table and ate two lunches.

Get Off My Property

During a location preparation day for an edgy art film, I had to distribute letters to every neighbor who was potentially going to be affected by our filming. We were asking these people of the high priced

Hollywood Hills area to sign a form either approving or disapproving our intrusion. It wasn't because the producers cared about these people's opinions, it was required by the permitting office.

During my travails throughout the neighborhood, I met all sorts of Hollywood types. Many were actors, a ton were directors, and bunches were producers.

Our big pitch to these affluent individuals to let us shoot days and nights outside their homes was that the director was actually one of their neighbors. He was one of them. Ideally, they would have all signed our permission slips with a big thumbs up chalking it up to comradery. But do things ever work that easily?

It's ironic. The people who are the least happy with filming in their neighborhoods are usually the same professionals who derive their lavish fortunes from the very business. This one feature film director, who lived right across the street from our future location, slammed his gate in my sweet smiling face as I explained how we were going to have to park a few trucks in front of his house. I almost lost a nose over that conversation.

The next house was full of cheery men. They told me to come back in a few hours when the homeowner returned. They assured me that their video producer friend would be cool about signing the form.

I came back a lot later and still the busy guy had not come home yet. The guys and I chatted a bit. They even wanted me to play Frisbee with them but I had to forge on and get more signatures. They guaranteed if I left the form, they'd see to it that it got approved. We agreed I could pick it up in the mailbox that night.

A couple of hours passed. It was getting very late and I was anxious to get home. I had finished up the last of the houses so I went over to the video producer's house and peeked inside the mailbox. There were a few bulky envelopes ready for a pick-up. I thumbed through the heap for my dinky little form. From out of nowhere, a head shot out from the dark.

"Who's there?!" he bellowed.

"I...I...I..." Oh dear. He thought I was a vandal trying to steal his mail. I apologized and laughed. He didn't find the situation as amusing as I did. His reaction was to yell at me—for harassing him!

Did I miss something? All I wanted was a stupid check mark on the stupid form. Agree or disagree. That was all. End of story.

All I wanted was a microwave dinner, a glass of milk, and a Valium. Who had the energy to harass this guy? Why didn't this creep ask the nice guys in his house how fun I was?

Before I could construct a sentence, he pulled out his cell phone and threatened to call the police if I did not get off his property immediately. I felt like I was in the Wild West and his cell phone was his modern replacement for a gun. I pulled out my cell phone and threatened to call the director.

"Oh yeah?" he taunted. "Then do it."

Damn, he called my bluff. I did the only reasonable thing I could think of. I sprinted to my car and peeled away.

Please Don't Send Me There!

As a production assistant, a person can see new sights, witness different ways of life, experience native tribal rituals, interact with the locals, and explore new horizons one never thought possible. All this without leaving the comforts of Los Angeles County.

"Alleyways. The most deplorable, squalid, filthy, vermin-infested alleyways are what I want!" bellowed the adamant director. Sure, he could be so confident about finding this kind of location. He wasn't the twenty-two-year-old white girl from the suburbs of quiet Northern California who had to go find these scary alleyways in the gangland of LA!

In truth, I didn't find these horrible alleys. A big buffed location scout named Jerry did that. After the director chose the most heinous one in all of Los Angeles, I spent the next day conducting a light test.

In other words, I had to be confined in the same spot for twelve hours in order to snap pictures periodically. This, of course, is to view how the sun shines on the location throughout the entire day's cycle. Let me tell you, those twelve hours can be the most eye opening experience of a lifetime.

Perhaps I should have seen this situation as an opportunity to study another facet of our very complicated world. Maybe I should have embraced the power of those people who had chosen the urban jungle way of life. Conceivably, I could have opened myself up to a world of different sights and smells foreign to my own life. Well—those smells stunk like rotting sewage.

I decided I was safer in the confines of my car. I had converted the inside of my Mustang convertible into a den. I had the Watchman going, the radio on, video games, piles of magazines, and loads of potato chips. I had it all going on, except I could have done without the silly disruptions of taking snapshots every fifteen minutes.

If you have never seen how many ways an alley can be used in downtown LA, I highly suggest you stay far, far away. I will never walk in a puddle again in my life if it hasn't rained that day! I now know the real meaning behind the term "squatters!"

Besides its neat functional use as a bathroom, did you know that alleys are a wonderful place to meet new people and sell white powder? And that's not all. It also serves as an after-school hangout for young people to enjoy the effects of underage smoking and alcohol consumption.

If you can't afford a hotel room, don't worry. Bring your hooker to the alley. If it's sleep you crave, there's always a refrigerator box waiting with your name on it.

The first thing I did when I got home was wash my hands and call my mother. She asked how everything went. Well, let's put it this way, at least I didn't witness any murders!

Later that month, the entire film crew went back to the same alley-way for two days of filming. Since I was the crew's most qualified site expert, I was assigned as the Pee Patrol Officer. My job was to make sure the passersby did not use our set as their toilet. Without training, how does one know proper Pee Patrol etiquette? Do you tell a bum to please go away before or after he's unzipped his fly?

CHAPTER TEN

Life's Little Itty-Bitty-Barely-Noticeable-I-Swear Mistakes

Okay, alright. I'll admit it. Sometimes we PAs are not perfect. Sometimes we make slight errors. Because of the extreme circumstances surrounding us, it's only natural that we occasionally falter a wee bit. After all, if the rest of Hollywood can run around like a bunch of dopes, PAs are allowed a little slack, right? Right?

Answering Phones

Before I started as a production assistant, I had never really had much experience with a busy office. Sure I had part-time jobs in hectic environments like bussing tables at a restaurant, sweeping popcorn grease off the movie theatre floors, and making smoothies for picky health nuts. However, nothing prepared me for a Hollywood production company's complicated telephone system and foreign telephone etiquette.

The phone rings, you answer it. Sure, it is an easy thing to do at home, but in a film production office it is **never** that simple.

After working a few days in a busy office, I came down with a serious disease—Phone Phobia. Not a good thing to have in a business that thrives on, is fueled by, could not even go three minutes without its telecommunication system. To this day, I sometimes get flashbacks and occasionally freak out when my telephone rings at home.

My first experience with all this technology was when I was working at a universally known studio's production company. This office was famous for putting out bad teenage flicks where the scantily clad women and their jock boyfriends always ended up having sex. Despite the fact that this company's films were nothing better than trash, the office was always tense. Apparently there was a lot of pressure to keep up their bad reputation.

The place was full of psychos, manic-depressives, and bitter recovering alcoholics. Then there was me, the sheltered college student watching these crazies whizzing by me in a highly caffeinated panic. Just being in their presence made me tremendously nervous. Yet, no matter how weird these people were, there was one man who was a hundred times worse. The producer.

We PAs did not see much, if any, of the man. Some PAs were convinced this producer did not even exist because he never came out of his office. A few of the PAs believed he was just a myth to keep the office afraid of slowing down its productivity. Those who knew the producer was real called him the "Screamer" because that's exactly what he did if he didn't like something.

I was one of the lucky few to know this man was indeed real. I could always hear him yelling behind the closed doors at his thirty-two-year-old male assistant. I don't know how his assistant could take that abuse every single day. I may not have known much about that office after only three weeks, but I sure as hell knew I could never work directly under a man like that. I shuddered at the thought.

One day I was reading a screenplay when I was hit with my greatest fear. The fear that haunted me so many times in recurring sweat drenched nightmares. The assistant announced to me that he would be taking a few days off and guess who was replacing him. Legally they couldn't make me do it, could they?

As far as I'm concerned, a phone should have twelve buttons—thirteen if it's really high-tech and has redial. As soon as a phone has a hold button, a speaker, flashing colored lights, and a headset, it becomes a frightening telephone system capable of all sorts of things like launching missiles from Guam.

After a brief (light speed) instruction session by the departing assistant about the phone and internet etiquette (etiquette?! I was lucky if I could turn the computer ON, let alone be able to do something that required any manners), I was left in the pit of darkness with the devil himself sitting in his office watching me through the glass wall that separated us.

The first phone call arrived. I answered it sweetly announcing that it was the producer's office. Without a polite "hello," a cordial "hi," or even a rushed "hey," a woman quickly blurted out her name. I could not understand her in her hastiness. Maybe she was nervous about talking to the producer so I kindly asked her to repeat herself.

She wasn't nervous, she was just conducting business as usual at Hollywood speed. Translation: she was way too pushy and needlessly stressed out to be polite.

I still could not understand her name after she repeated it, but I knew she'd yell at me if I did not patch her through to the boss guy immediately. Now, as if life wasn't complicated enough, instead of verbally announcing this candidate for heart disease to the producer, I had to use a horribly complicated machine called the Amtel. It's a mini keyboard and screen on which you type a message and send it to the big man's office electronically. Between the computer, the phone, and the Amtel, I was screwed.

I typed in this incomprehensible name and prayed the Screamer recognized who she was with a few key letters. I closed my eyes, crossed my fingers and held my breath hoping he wouldn't started yelling at me. It's no wonder his assistant took off work eagerly for a week's worth of jury duty. If I were this guy's permanent assistant, I would have demanded to be put on the O.J. Simpson trial.

Miraculously, the producer recognized the caller. By way of his own Standard American Screamer Sign Language, he made gestures resembling those of an umpire throwing a player out of a game. I understood this signal to mean he wanted the woman's call put through to him. And so I did.

At that instant, I fully understood why he was honored with his nickname. He threw the glass door open and stood two inches from my face while he yelled profanities at me alphabetically until his throat went dry around the letter Q. Then, with his face flaming red, he demanded I get him some water so he could keep going to the letter Z.

The actual message he was trying to signal with his arms flailing like a chimpanzee was that he would call the *Studio Executive* back later. In fact, he had been trying to avoid her call for days because he didn't have a finished script for her yet. He explained how I had made him "look like a fool."

Trust me, he was doing a superb job on his own.

Okay, I felt humiliated, hurt, and thoroughly degraded but that didn't stop the phone from ringing. This time it was his four-year-old daughter. Why he was blessed with reproductive skills is beyond me. I typed over to him who it was via that stupid Amtel. He smiled and signaled for me to patch his kid through.

For *some* reason the phone wouldn't allow me to connect them. Instead, it dumped his daughter and put me on the line with him. He started calling me his little darling sweetheart and asked me how I was. I figured he was trying to apologize for his earlier outburst. I told him I was fine and thanked him.

Suffice it to say, I was giving this man way too much credit for his personality disorder. He was, let's just say, less than thrilled to hear my voice. Through the glass I saw his unnatural smile turn sour. His face twisted up like a tornado taking on a house as he asked who the hell he was talking to.

He turned to me through the window with this horrendous expression similar to what a murder victim might see of his killer right before being strangled to death. I tried to duck but I couldn't fit under the desk. Instead, I was forced to look at him and smile like an idiot.

He slammed the phone down so hard they could hear the plastic SMASH all the way to the next studio. It was the first time in my life I was responsible for someone breaking a telephone.

Rebel Without a Map

Donald was young. Donald was fun. Donald was wild. He was free. He was alive. He was a production assistant with the keys to the company's Lincoln Towncar. Donald was stylin'.

It was an early June morning. As the sun was rising above the Malibu Hills, Donald was cruising in the Towncar with the stereo blasting. It isn't very often that a producer gives a PA the keys to a brand new car to go pick up one of the world's most prestigious actors. And Donald was not about to let the opportunity slip away.

As much fun as he was having, he kept rehashing the producer's insinuations that Donald could mess something this easy up. Actually the producer said: "Don't $#&! this up—or else that actor will have both of our butts on a platter!"

The producer hated Donald ever since he was forced to take the kid on as a favor to his brother-in-law. It made it that much more important for Donald to prove what a great PA he was.

The affluent neighborhood was still asleep after a long night of counting their millions. Ah, Donald couldn't wait to fill his mattress full of money someday. Until then, he was content being the driver of one of the highest paid, most temperamental dramatic actors in the business.

Getting to the actor's house had been a cinch. It was finding the film's location site hidden deep in the San Fernando Valley that posed a slight problem. When the actor questioned Donald's directional abilities, Donald was sly. He promised the actor that he knew a short cut.

Before long, Donald had gotten them completely lost. He had no idea what city they were in. Fortunately, the actor had stayed up way too late the night before hosting a charity for some endangered moth and hadn't bothered to learn any of his lines. The actor stayed quiet in the backseat with the script two centimeters from his face while Donald silently went crazy in the driver's seat.

It was 7 a.m. The actor was expected in make-up in a half hour. The set was located in a remote area in Reseda and Donald was too proud to have brought the map. At the rate he was going, the set might as well have been five thousand miles away.

The count down was on. Twenty-two minutes to go and Donald kept finding himself coming to dead end streets.

The minutes kept ticking by and the actor kept growling as he flubbed lines. Blue veins appeared on Donald's forehead. Beads of sweat fell into his eyes almost blinding him.

Fifteen minutes and counting with still no clue where they were. The actor looked up in confusion and demanded to know how much longer it was going to take. Donald had no answer except: "Almost there."

With each gas station they passed, Donald winced in agony. How easy it would be to stop for directions—but that would be giving in and looking like a total moron. Plus, it would get back to the producer who would've happily fired Donald.

It was 7:21 a.m. Well, this was it—Donald was about to admit he messed up when the actor piped in, "Thank God for Starbucks. Pop in and espresso me."

Donald found the Lord that day.

Twenty-five minutes later Donald delivered the actor *fashionably late*. The producer sprinted over to the Towncar ready to beat Donald to a pulp. Donald closed his eyes in fear.

Just then the actor let out a big, "Aaahhh! It's good to be alive."

Everyone on the set turned in disbelief. Who was that man? Surely it couldn't be their actor who never smiled before noon.

Suddenly no one cared about Donald's tardiness. A caffeinately content actor was more than anyone could have hoped for. Even the producer was impressed with whatever it was Donald did. He shook Donald's hand and said, "Good work, son. I knew I could count on you."

That afternoon, Donald bought a map and intently studied every single street in Los Angeles County.

Loose Lips

Jacey had always been well loved and respected. Everyone at work ceaselessly thought she was a marvelous office PA. She was a petite, freckled young woman with a face that said 'trust me,' and a giggle full of pure innocence. She never had trouble making friends because she was a terrific listener. And on one very high-stress film shoot, an entire crew looked to her as a trusted ear.

Jacey was quick to comfort anyone coming through the production office who was having a bad day—which was just about every single person on any given day thanks to the Nazi regime running the film. The unhappiness from the top quickly trickled all the way down the chain of command and landed in Jacey's lap to console.

When things were slow in the production office, she'd play therapist to the hapless movie crew souls in the lunch room. Her "patients" would lay down on the couch and spill their guts to this twenty-two-year-old Mother Goose-type.

Before long, Jacey was getting all the best gossip on everyone. She knew who was sleeping with whom, who wasn't getting any, who absolutely sucked at it, who had to pay for it, who was the biggest scum bag in the world to work for, who was having marital problems, who was a lush, and who was an addict. You know, the usual office defamation.

After a few weeks into this agonizing shoot, people opened up even more to Jacey. Laurie, the production coordinator, came crying to Jacey about how she utterly despised Bob and Jon, her two assistant production coordinators, because they were lazy, good-for-nothings who got the job only because of nepotism. (They were related to the director of photography's lawyer's mistress.)

Then, not knowing that Laurie had finished a session thirty minutes prior, Bob and Jon came whining to Jacey about how they wanted to squeeze Laurie's pinhead right off. They complained she was such a weasel and treated them like children.

Jacey didn't really care what the reasons were, she just loved hearing all the gossip. However, as time passed, the tension began to intensify between the feuding coordinators. That's when Jacey found herself stuck in the middle of way more than a fun little game of Freudian role-playing.

Each side thought Jacey was rooting for them. All poor, little Jacey wanted in life was to buy the world a Coke and sing in perfect harmony...and listen to more gossip.

But this was getting way out of control. After any given blowout between the three coordinators, each of them would get Jacey alone for her opinion on the situation. Her only opinion was that she didn't want to lose her job. So she did the only thing she could—she played the yes-man to all of them.

Bob and Jon appreciated Jacey's "honesty" and took her out for drinks. She was so excited. Maybe things were going to be okay after all. There were seven weeks left of this horrible movie and then it would all be over, she sighed with relief. She hoped she, Bob, Jon, and Laurie could all be friends and hang out on weekends after everything had blown over.

That evening, Bob and Jon wined and dined Jacey. They were having a great time boozing it up with drinking games and a near disastrous round of drunken darts. It didn't take long for tiny Jacey to feel the impact of the alcoholic punch.

Bob and Jon carefully noted her insobriety and smiled at how cute she was. Like wild hyenas, the two men took the opportunity to pounce upon their inebriated prey. The questions flew at once. They wanted to know all the dirt on Laurie. What had she told Jacey? What did Laurie say about the two of them? Was Laurie plotting against them? More importantly, what were Laurie's weaknesses?

Of course Jacey knew all of Laurie's self-professed shortcomings—like how she cheated on her petty cash expense reports every month and how she occasionally stole handfuls of stamps each week. She knew how Laurie tried to get Bob and Jon fired although it obviously hadn't worked and what really ticked her off when it came to these guys.

For a moment, Jacey had complete clarity of what she was thinking. She couldn't let these guys know what was said between two women in confidence.

But Bob and Jon were her friends.

But she wasn't a Benedict Arnold. Forget it. She wasn't going to say a word.

However, somehow that stream of conscious thinking was intercepted and tackled to the ground by another tequila. Her mouth became a floodgate of information that was instantaneously pulled W-I-D-E open. She began to talk so fast that the guys had to ask her to repeat herself.

No, she thought. She wouldn't repeat herself. Yet, she found herself spelling it on napkins.

On Monday, Jacey sat at her desk thinking about what an awful subhuman being she was. What were those guys going to do to Laurie? The dead silence in the office was unbearable. She wished someone would just yell at her and tell her how horrible she was.

Laurie pulled Jacey aside. Oh no, Jacey's life was over. Laurie was sure to have heard how she betrayed her. She'd never talk to Jacey again. Even worse, she'd never hire Jacey on another film. Hello burning bridges, Jacey thought as Laurie led her to the "therapy room."

Instead of yelling, Laurie started talking a mile a minute. She was delirious with depraved happiness. She knew how she could get Bob and Jon fired—finally! She caught them cheating on their timecards and mileage log. Ha! She had them right where she wanted them!

All of a sudden, Jacey's mouth opened uncontrollably. She told Laurie exactly what Bob and Jon *really* do when she wasn't in the office. They watched television, made long distance phone calls, and even went through Laurie's purse and desk.

Jacey wanted to hide her head in the sand.

Laurie was so upset with the guys. Within three seconds, World War Three had exploded right there inside the production office.

Aaahhh! Jacey hit herself. She was a gossip junkie that seriously needed professional help. Where was *her* therapist?

Now what? They were all going to kill each other and Jacey was to blame. She felt like a Japanese warrior who had failed his countrymen. The only right thing to do was kill herself for causing such destruction. She raised a letter opener to her heart. Oh, this was going to hurt. Maybe she could just quit the job she loved so much and risk never getting another PA job again. Her name would be mud in this town. She started designing her new nametag.

But before she could go on, the production manager rushed to see what all the commotion was about. With a blink of his eyes, he canned all three of the coordinators on the spot. He had been sick of them all for months.

With three instant openings, guess who became the newest assistant production coordinator?

Thrilled with her new promotion, Jacey decided to give up her therapy side job. Yeah, right—*that* idea lasted almost a whole hour.

Ambling Around

Simon, a newly hired office PA for a major production company was excited. Why was he so excited? Well, besides getting a decent paying job straight out of college, he was working at a tremendously famous company run by two of the most impressive names in Hollywood. Plus, the company was a week away from releasing a monstrously epic film. Simon couldn't believe his luck. But it got even better than that—the boss was on vacation *and* the office was closed for a three-day weekend while the carpets were being replaced.

Of all the weekends, his old hometown friends happened to pick that lucky one to visit. Simon was thrilled at the chance to show them around his turf. Alright, let's face it, he couldn't wait to blow his friends away with all his inside access to Hollywood.

When Simon picked them up at the airport on Friday morning, his friends thought they'd be doing the usual tourist stuff like the Walk of Fame and the beach. No way, Simon had much greater plans for them. He took them directly to work.

Since the rest of Universal Studios was working like usual, a studio guard welcomed their arrival. Simon flashed his identification and the guard ushered them through. The friends oohed and ahhed at how cool Simon was to let them go where few civilians have ever gone before.

While his friends were still dumbfounded by just being inside a real studio, Simon drew a borrowed set of keys to the company's golf cart out of his pocket. With a devilish grin, he told his pals to hop into "his" golf cart.

All four of the friends piled into the two-man golf cart faster than you can say, "nose job." Simon flipped on his mega-hip Hollywood shades while his small town friends ate it up. They were cool just for being friends with this totally hip stud.

Away they chugged as Simon secretly tried to get the hang of the cart. He had only used it one other time to run an errand on the lot.

Unfortunately that errand didn't go very well because he nearly wiped out two pedestrians. But that was not a story any of his pals needed to hear.

After stalling a couple of times and blaming it on the terribly low grade gas they filled the tank with, Simon soon became a pro at driving the little cart. In no time, they were whipping their way through the studio's plentiful backlot as the Santa Ana winds blew through their hair.

Occasionally, an old chunky tram or two full of tourists would pass by. The tourists ogled at the four "insiders" with jealousy. Even though they had no idea who Simon and his three friends were, the trams full of people lapped up the excitement.

Cameras flashed from every direction. Camcorders focused in on this cool bunch of movers and shakers. Simon and his buddies waved and hammed it up for their crowds of adoring fans.

This was great PR for the studio, Simon thought to himself. His bosses should revere him as a marketing king. He should get a cut of the theme park's profits for at least the day. Maybe he'd ask for a raise Monday morning. He was on his way to becoming someone big. He just hoped none of his co-workers were spending the day anywhere in earshot.

Up and down the hills they zoomed. Simon's friends were as happy as little five-year-old kids as they passed the *Back to the Future* clock tower and the Beaver's house. Simon couldn't let the fun end. He had to outdo himself from the last spectacle. So, off to the *Psycho* house they barreled.

From inside the famed, off-limits shower set of the Hitchcock classic, Simon and his friends waved at the unfortunate public who would never, ever, ever be able to hop the tram rail that separated the dreamers from the tinsel town elite.

Simon was lost in his own little reverie imagining the incredible things people from his hometown would be saying about him for years. He was so awesome. He was the Man. He was AHHH!…in the path of an oncoming two hundred thousand ton tram with a take-no-prisoners driver on a strict schedule. All four of the friends looked something like Janet Leigh in the famed shower scene as they headed straight for the tram's front-end grill.

Forget the *Jaws* exhibition. This was much more terrifying because no one can hear you scream over the piercing banshee squeals of a fifty-year-old tram grinding its brakes at full speed.

Simon clumsily jerked the cart off the path and into the muddy soft shoulder, out of harm's way. The tram came to a grating dead stop. Simon and the gruff tram driver looked at each other in shock and terror. The friends were checking to see if their limbs were not broken while the tourists gaped at the commotion.

The tram driver's panic turned into a sour look of hatred. His face turned into a mess of squints and wrinkles as his lips grumbled with a deep penetrating roar. Simon tried to cover his idiocy with a chuckle hoping the tram driver could find the humor in all of it. No such luck. The old man started swearing like a maniac with a horrendous case of Tourette Syndrome. Mothers covered their children's ears while everyone else captured the Kodak moment forever.

All Simon knew was that they needed to get the hell out of there while they had all of their body parts intact. He gunned the sputtering motor, but the cart's wheels spun hopelessly. Mud was spraying everywhere. The tram operator started to take off his seat belt to demonstrate his road rage on Simon's head.

Simon was ready to jump out of the cart and run like the wind but that wasn't a story he wanted to hear repeated back at his old barber shop. Finally, with the help of some sort of divine intervention, we'll just call it divine traction, the cart was able to haul itself out of the embankment. The friends drove away faster than a flea can hop—or at least faster than a crippled donkey. Fortunately for them, the old tram driver wasn't in peak physical condition, and besides it was specifically specified in his union contract that he didn't have to leave the driver's seat unless there was a donut involved.

About eight dozen video cameras followed their dramatic departure. Although they were a good distance away. Simon and his buddies could hear the crowd loudly applauding their much-appreciated performance.

Spooling the Film

It was my fourth week as a PA at a production company at a high profiled studio. I was confident about what I was doing. I knew the lot and I knew the lingo. I was going places in my brand new Jaguar. Actually I was going to the car wash with the boss' new Jaguar.

After that errand was accomplished, I hopped into my own slightly aged, slightly dinged, slightly faded Ford. I was feeling good about my new career in Hollywood. Soon I would own this town, I said to myself as I adjusted my cool new sunglasses.

However, before I could conquer anything, I first had to pick up the master print of the company's soon-to-be-released comedy film. I was instructed to guard that film with my life. I assured the office folks that they had nothing to worry about with me on the case.

At the screening room, the editor had finished showing the film to all the studio bigwigs who had given their final approval on the film. This was an exciting moment for me. I could feel the creative energy in the room. I felt like I belonged. When I walked in, the editor glared at me and said, "Who the hell are you?"

Regardless, I had my instructions and I was going to see that I followed them through.

I brought the film back to the studio where I handed it off to the assistant editor, Ellie. Yeah, mission accomplished. I was too wonderful for words.

Ellie asked me if I wanted to get my hands on some film. Finally, someone could see that all I needed was a chance to prove my extraordinary filmic talents.

I had never held real 35mm motion picture film before, let alone been allowed to take part in the editing process. So of course I jumped at the chance, though I was smooth about it. I didn't want to seem like a novice.

Ellie told me to manually rewind the thick spool of the 35mm sound roll. She explained this audio would later be married to the visuals. I spooled the reel ever so gently. This was a piece of cake; even a duck could do it. If this was what editing was all about—yawn—I needed a profession with a little more excitement, like say, directing.

But I kept my opinions to myself and continued spinning. I didn't want Ellie to think I was ungrateful for the chance to learn about her boring job.

However, what I expected to be a project worthy of maybe ten, fifteen minutes tops was taking much longer. Maybe this wasn't as quick as it appeared. But it wasn't hard at all. In fact with a little oomph of the spool, the roll practically rewound itself. If only Ellie could have seen me, she would have been so impressed that she would have hired me to be on her team. Unfortunately she had gone into the other room to work on something else.

I cranked up the music a little louder as I spun the reel with gusto. I was a dancing party animal. Let's face it, I was an editing champion.

Everything was going well until, all of a sudden, the spool of film went bonkers (no fault of my own, I swear) and uncontrollably spun right off the wheel.

I grabbed the turning crank to slow it down but there was this thing involving the laws of Physics by which the roll was possessed. My unexpected jerking stop made the audio/film roll snap like a twig.

I almost died. How could I have messed up something so trivial and in such a huge way. This was the audio track that everyone in the world was going to listen to in the theatres. Oh my GOD. What was I going to do?!

Well, for starters, I quickly pulled my sunglasses off.

Then I panicked. Could they sue me? Should I run away? Should I fall on the floor and pretend an alien life form had tried to kill me in order to sabotage the film? No, they might steal my idea, make it into a movie of the week and never give me any credit or royalties.

I swallowed my pride and ran to Ellie for help. She calmly assessed the damage and then started to panic. Fortunately she was not the loud screaming type. She just started chewing her nails to the nub.

We carefully rolled the film back into two smaller rolls so we could evaluate how bad the tear was. She smoothed out the sound track and taped the two ends together. We both looked at each other and gulped as she put the track on the sound machine.

Okay, this was it. This was the moment I would see which of the actors was going to pummel me to death for ruining their line. Ellie said a silent prayer and played the broken audio track. I am not sure how this happened, but somehow I managed to break the strip during a slight pause in dialogue. It went something like this:

Actress in a Valley girl accent: "You're such, like…" (there's a pause while she tries to think of an insult.)

TEAR in the audio track

Actress: "…a stupid ass."

We both sighed a great relief that the actress' dynamic performance and profound dialogue were not harmed. I collapsed onto the floor clutching my heart. Ellie told me never to show my face in her office again. She had herself a deal!

Can We Talk?

Adrienne was a production assistant on a late night talk show. She absolutely loved her job. On a regular basis, she substituted for the receptionist during lunch. Of all the cool things she did all day, this was by far her most beloved part of the job. Sitting at that front desk was like having the best seat in the house at the world's strangest freak show.

There was no telling who was going to call or walk through those big glass doors at any given time.

Honestly, no one can really know how large the population of certifiably insane lunatics is out there in Los Angeles until one sits at a desk like this.

Everyday the phone would ring and maybe three out of ten calls would be some schmo trying to convince Adrienne that he or she needed to talk to the talk show host. "And who may I say is calling?" Adrienne would humor them by asking.

"I'm his sister/ brother/ wife/ mother/ analyst," they would respond with dead seriousness.

"I'm sorry, he's busy at the moment. I'll be happy to take your name and number," she would say as they either hung up or carried on the joke by supplying their real information. Adrienne pretended to write everything down as she read her magazine.

Other times people would call into the main switchboard and tell her they were John Travolta's agent or Dolly Parton. Adrienne was most impressed with those who at least attempted to sound legitimate. She had fun with impersonators who tried to even book themselves onto the show.

"Sure, what day are you available?" Adrienne would muse before telling them, "Whoops, we're booked that day. Call again later."

One time a frazzled woman called claiming she was Ed McMahon's assistant and lost the number to the talk show host's assistant. Adrienne was getting a kick out of this woman's amusingly convincing performance.

"I have Mr. McMahon sitting next to me. May he please speak with the talk show host?" the woman asked frantically.

"One moment," Adrienne said as she put the woman on hold while she finished the remainder of an article on the latest bikini fashions. After a couple of minutes, Adrienne got back on the line and said, "I'm sorry. All the lines are busy. Can I take down your name and number?"

Adrienne could hear the woman mumble something to another person on the other end. A man mumbled back. He kind of did sound like Ed. Their act was pretty good, but Adrienne was not going to fall for the old Ed McMahon calling the switchboard routine.

The woman came back on the line disappointed and flustered. She said, "Okay then. I guess we'll try back later."

Another poor sap trying to be somebody in this town, Adrienne thought. At least they were pretty decent actors.

A few moments later, Adrienne's boss rushed over to her and said that Ed McMahon should have called by now. Her boss figured that Mr. McMahon's assistant might have lost the direct phone number.

Her boss said, "Adrienne, if Ed McMahon calls, you'll send him straight through. Right?"

Adrienne shrank to the size of a worm. "Of course I will."

CHAPTER ELEVEN

Fans—Sometimes They Are Not Cool

When non-entertainment people—you know those who think movies just *happen* on a screen—visit the "real" world of production, it's always a hazard. It's kind of like putting an ex-monk into a room full of Playboy bunnies.

Basically, the same thing happens when an average person finds out his or her favorite actor is starring in a project being shot in their neighborhood. You may as well pull out the protective armor right away because otherwise you're not getting out of there alive.

Fan-atical

I was working on a star-studded film with world-renowned comedians. The cast alone was worth three-quarters of the exorbitant budget. Once neighbors got wind of their presence, they went crazy. They did anything they could to try and fondle the actors or at least get a body part signed.

I tried to stay as far away from the hoopla as possible but I enjoyed watching the teenage girls accost the actors' trailers. I felt sorry for the actor's personal assistants who were trying to hold the teens back. I made the mistake of running in to help. From out of nowhere, a woman lunged at me. Her eyes were red and puffy. She had a hard time getting her words out in complete sentences. After a long moment of gasping for air, she said she was promised an autographed picture of our most famous actor.

My reaction was, "Yeah, so?" Please, did she really think I could do anything about it? Oh sure, let me just pull an autographed picture out of thin air for this stranger. I couldn't even get one for my own mother, and I had history with this actor—he stepped on my foot once.

Was it my fault if a highly self-involved actor was too busy to sign an autograph on command? Well, apparently some non-movie folks thought it was.

Okay, okay. It wasn't this lady's fault for falling for this actor's publicists' hype. She was only human and needed an icon to cling to, even if that international icon was a pain in the ass.

Knowing that she wasn't going to be satisfied leaving empty handed, I let her touch the actor's trailer door while he was far, far away from the set. She rubbed her face against the handle. She licked the doorknob. And finally she sniffed the steps. She was so grateful that she left without another thought about the silly autographed picture.

The Autograph or Your Life

We were filming out on location in Nevada at a squalid tow truck yard. It was a super sized movie starring an actor who's best known for his choice roles as white trash.

It was hard keeping ourselves inconspicuous with all the lights and trucks on the normally barren industrial streets. As soon as the word got out about our celebrity's presence, people came from high and low to get a glimpse.

I hate to say it, but this guy's fans were some of the ugliest people I've ever seen.

One sixty-year-old woman in particular was dressed in a moo-moo and slippers. Her name was Norma and she was as large as a mid-sized sedan. She easily shoved her way through the crowds and past our wooden barricades that were designed to separate us Hollywoodites from the common folk. Norma, with her chin full of thick stubble and a mouth that would make a truck driver blush, wouldn't stand to be segregated from her favorite movie star.

She was sweating and shaking with delirium. She quivered, nearly inaudibly, "Can I meet him?"

It wasn't hard to figure out which *him* she wanted to meet. By the looks of her, Norma was probably straight out of some trailer park from the nearby desert. We couldn't let this mad woman frothing at the mouth meet the actor. If we had, she would have scared the sleaze-pot-typecast star into becoming a respectable screen sex-god.

Anthony, the cool, calm, always collected second assistant director, told the nearly toothless Norma that he would happily take her name and address. He promised to *try* and send her an autographed picture **after** the film was wrapped. That was enough to keep her swearing and crying with happiness for hours. Fortunately she kept plenty of tissue hidden in her bosom.

Two weeks later, I was back in our LA office recouping from the location heavy shoot. The worst of it was over. I had my feet up on the desk, grooving to some tunes pretending to take care of production issues when the phone rang. It was Norma, the queen of trailer trash and Jerry Springer's number one fan. I was shocked she had found our number. She hadn't struck me as a resourceful type.

It turned out that she threatened to sit on Jason, our little PA, if he didn't give her the telephone number. I'd call that resourceful!

The first thing she had to say to me was how despicable Anthony was for being such a liar and how our whole company was full of big, fat &%#!-ing liars. Then she told me how we movie people should all &%#!-ing burn in hell for all our lies we filled the world with daily, except Jerry Springer. Then she threatened to come after Anthony if she didn't get the autograph soon.

In the middle of her threatening speech, she asked, "Oh hey, could you hang on? I've got another call."

"No problem," I said. I had nothing better to do.

"Thanks, your the &%#!-ing best, hon," she praised.

When she returned, she continued to preach on about how we movie people were part of the conspiracy to hide evidence of life from outer space. I told her she was probably right.

"You're not &%#!-ing listening to me, are you?" she yelled. "I'm going to kill Anthony if I don't get my autographed picture. Oh yeah, and my parole officer says she wants one too. Can you do that for me? Thanks hon, you're the &%#!-ing best."

CHAPTER TWELVE

The Things We Do for Love (and because we have no choice)

Sometimes there's no rhyme or reason why things happen to production assistants. There are just certain uncertainties to this crazy business that we love so much.

Whatever it is, one thing is for sure, a PA is one of the most well rounded employees in the job market thanks to hundreds of random skills he or she will acquire throughout the years.

Unfortunately, most of these newfound skills are useless to anyone in real life.

Gardening Their Way to Fame

Peter and Lyle were a couple of fun loving production assistants at the office of a well-respected comedy writer/ director/ producer named Arthur. It was a slow Friday; nothing particularly exciting was going on in the world of comedy.

The phone rang, disturbing the guys' naps. Peter wiped the drool off his face and answered it. On the other end was a woman sobbing hysterically. Peter could not understand a word she was babbling. He put her on speaker phone so Lyle could also enjoy her wild hysteria. The two guys looked at each other and whispered, "It's the wife."

Peter put the tearful, mumbling woman on hold and intercommed Arthur. "Sir, your wife is on the phone…crying again."

His response was expected: "Oh Christ! What's the [bleepity bleeping] catastrophe today?!"

Suffice it to say, this woman was born whining over something. Arthur often joked behind his wife's back that if she were to die in the middle of one of her temper tantrums, he was going to have her clenched body stuffed and mounted above his mantle—so he could throw things at her. He was constantly talking about leaving her, but after seven years of marriage he knew that even divorce wouldn't put a cork in her.

He always told people that when he started out as a writer, he was perfectly content working at home. But after six weeks of marriage to this hell raiser, he decided to pursue a career directing and producing as well so he could spend *less* time at home.

Arthur took his wife's call as Peter and Lyle pressed their ears to his office door. One might think Arthur would have yelled at his wife to quit her griping. Instead, all he ever said was, 'Yes dear,' 'Okay honey,' 'Yes sweetheart,' 'Anything you want,' and 'I love you too, pumpkin.'

This got Peter and Lyle every time. They fell to the floor in hysterics. How ironic that this man had the tongue of a snake and the claws of a tiger when it came to dealing with people on a business level, but with his wife he was as timid as a newly neutered puppy.

A few moments later Arthur came out of his office looking like he lost an alley fight with the entire World Wresting Federation.

"Hey guys," he said haggardly to Peter and Lyle. "I need you to help me." He was a really cool boss so Peter and Lyle were always happy to help their compadre, especially for the sake of Guyhood.

Arthur explained, "The gardeners couldn't make it and my wife's having her monthly garden party. Go to my house and make friends with the gardening equipment. Trust me, she'll tell you **exactly** what she needs."

And that she did. She probably would have made a great director if she ever had the initiative to work.

Peter and Lyle spent four hours planting, weed whacking, grass mowing, furniture arranging, dog grooming and while-you're-at-it house repairs. When they were finished, Arthur's wife offered to pay them nothing more than one Pepsi Cola each. Despite her chintzy recompense, she thought the two guys were better than the invention of daytime television.

"These two boys are faaaabulous," she boasted to her tea party playmates. "I'm going to have you both back to put up the Christmas lights that outline the entire house. Do you do house painting as well? Where did my husband find you two handymen?"

One of her friends piped in, "You know my husband could use a hand putting up a fence. Are you boys available Saturday?"

Peter and Lyle looked at each other. Oh yes, they were going places in Hollywood.

The Cyan Shoe Diaries

Frank got the call from Lane who couldn't take the gig off Sonia's hands. Frank was happy to take the work even if it was only two days worth.

This time it was a commercial for some hair dye. Cool. Easy money while watching some famous model-turned-primetime-actress flip her locks a million times claiming how great she looked.

"How hard could this be?" Frank laughed to himself.

We're talking A) no crowd control, B) no exterior shots in the broiling sun, C) no loud neighbors to contend with, and D) not even a big stage to patrol. Only a beautiful woman sitting in a chair in front of a blue background.

Frank grazed through the craft service table contemplating why he was even needed on the set. Everything appeared to be unnaturally calm and under control. However, before he could take off his jacket, the disheveled second assistant director popped out of nowhere right in front of Frank's face. She shot him a strange look and whooped like some sort of African bird, "You Jack?"

"Frank. I'm—," he tried.

"Uh, yeah, whatever," she said unconcerned. "You're being summoned to the wardrobe trailer ASAP. They needed you like last year."

Frank didn't have to travel far into the base camp's trailer park to figure out where wardrobe was stationed. Female screams of bloody murder were a pretty good indication he was getting close.

He stopped at the noisy trailer and stuck out his beefy chest. He smiled boldly. Ah yes, this could be his chance to live out his lifelong male fantasy of rescuing a beautiful model in distress. He could picture the whole scene unfolding in front of him. He'd rip the door off the trailer. His buttons would burst open to reveal a peek of his pecks. He would find the gorgeous woman heaving, frightened over something trivial like a little spider. Her weakness would make him love her even more. He would take her into his arms, kill the evil spider, and she would kiss him all over…

He opened the door to find no model, no actress, no spider, and no need for his shirt to be undone. Instead he found Melissa, a wispy, mousy brown-haired wardrobe assistant covered in blue dye. Her face, her hands and clothes were all stained. But she was kind of cute, Frank thought.

When she saw Frank, she threw herself into his freshly cleaned, crisp white shirt with the weight of an elephant. "You have no idea how much I need you right now," she whispered in his ear.

Hmmm, he could really get to like this job. He realized how suspicious his new blue appearance would look to the rest of the crew, but he considered it his prize—his proof of conquest, one might say.

Melissa pulled herself away from Frank who was holding her in a vice grip. She explained how she needed to dye a pair of dainty high heeled shoes that were to be worn by the actress/model in exactly two hours and 14 minutes. She had to get them to perfectly match a cyan colored scarf.

Frank was desperately trying to take this all in, but he didn't get it. He looked at Melissa softly, as though he was saving the day, and said, "The shoes and the scarf look the same color to me."

He might as well have lit a stick of dynamite.

"Ahhhhh!" Melissa screamed with the capacity of someone much taller and blonder than herself. "You are such a GUY!"

Frank figured that wasn't a compliment.

"The scarf is cyan. The shoes are ocean. Ocean, *duh*, is way too close to royal than I want. You can't tell the diff? What are you, color blind?"

Okay, he was starting to dislike this girl.

He looked at the shoes, looked at his stained shirt, looked at Melissa weeping and quivering like a little frail flower in the corner. He felt awful for her. He was ready to blow this emotional warp and go get himself some breakfast.

Then, as if the clouds parted to reveal a full moon, the werewolf in Melissa awoke to expose its razor sharp teeth. She grabbed him by his collar with her claws rendering him immobile. "You are not leaving me, buddy boy."

That's when he remembered the vow he made to himself years ago to never speak with the female of the human species. This was a woman with serious shoe issues and now she had a production assistant to sacrifice. He felt powerless. He was sweating. He was kind of getting turned on.

"Okay," she said, "you've got two hours to find this color shoe with a wide three inch heel in size eight narrow. I don't care if they are leather, velvet or suede. Do not get jelly or plastic because the actress/model will eat us alive if her feet can't breathe properly. You have a pager, right?"

Check! Pager waiting for its cue. That was the only thing he honestly understood from her little epitaph. Did she seriously think he could handle this mission? How was he supposed to go shopping for something of such great importance? Especially when the only time he ever got new clothes was when they mysteriously appeared in his closet after his mom came to visit.

All he could choke from his vocal chords was, "But, but, but…"

Could she do this to him? Did this mean he wasn't going to get anything to eat until this was accomplished?

Was he going to get to meet the incredibly hot actress/model babe and personally slip her adorable feet into whatever shoes he bought for her?

He'd be a hero. A god. A film stud. Life was good again. He shuttered in great passion. That fantasy was enough to keep him going without even so much as a snack until lunch.

When Frank arrived at the mall, he instinctively looked for any chair near a dressing room. Wait a minute—it suddenly dropped on him like a ton of stale salami. He had to do the shopping and there was only one hour and fifty-one minutes left.

Ooh, Saks was having a sale on boots. Nordstrom probably had a good variety of suede. Perhaps Neiman would be able to recommend a decent pump.

AHHH! What was happening to him?!

Seven stores later, there was only one remote possibility. It was a cobalt sandal that was nowhere near the shade of the cyan scarf. His pager went off. He leaped out of his seat in Bloomingdale's footwear department and ran to call Melissa. After ten minutes searching for a telephone, he was able to reach the production office who in turn had to hunt down Melissa's boss who had to get a production assistant to find Melissa.

She chirped eagerly, "Did you find anything yet? You realize we only have forty-seven minutes, don't you?" Apparently she didn't realize how much time she was sucking up by paging him.

He ducked into a cheapie shoe store, the last shoe source in the entire mall. Low and behold, before him stood the world's biggest rainbow assortment of plastic shoes. He paced up and down the blue shoe aisle. He needed to be a hero to Melissa. More importantly, he had to please the goddess of the blonde hair dye.

As if a light from heaven were leading him to it, he found a size 81/2 wide stiletto CYAN synthetic pump. With twenty-one minutes to get back to the set, he had no other choice but to plunk down the money and run.

He dodged the Los Angeles traffic like a mad man running from a straight-jacket and squealed into the stage's parking lot with six minutes to spare. He was panting like a dog with his tongue hanging out his mouth. He knew he was going to get hell for the shoes being the wrong size but he was more worried about the actress/model having a cow over them not being leather.

He found a marking pen in a nearby trailer and delicately scribbled out the words stamped on the heel that said MAN MADE MATERIAL. He put the shoes back in the box and approached the stage.

Where was everyone? He expected the whole crew would be gathered around outside awaiting his arrival like a hunter bringing back the goods. Well…maybe they'd be gathered on the set ready to chant his name. Frank! Frank! Frank!

Inside the stage, Frank saw the actress/model smiling and shaking her head for the camera. But how could they start filming without the shoes?

"Oh, you're back. *Finally*," Melissa said preoccupied with the scene. He puckered up. Where was the kiss?

"We decided a chartreuse would make a much better contrast to her dress. It shows off the hair better."

Melissa might as well have punched him in the gut. There wasn't going to be a big hero's welcome. Poor Frank drowned his sorrow in bagels.

'Tis the Season

The holiday season always brings out the generosity in everyone— even the stingiest, most backbiting executives.

Despite any religious affiliation, Hollywood's production offices are always illuminated with twinkling lights, aromatic Christmas trees/ Hanukah bushes and seasonal treats with the Los Angeles temperatures dipping into the bone chilling low-70's. Brrrrr!

That extra special time of year starts around December 1st when everyone comes back from the Thanksgiving belly stuffing-fest and discovers this is when the **real** work of the year begins.

First, the producers, directors, and studio executives have to pull out their extended list of contacts. This information is usually found on the computer because no Rolodex in the world is big enough to fit all these people's "friend's" names. Inevitably, it will be this same computer that will faithfully crash before the information is properly executed onto those annoying labels.

And don't even think you can save time by handwriting these labels. That would look sloppy and unprofessional in the eyes of the gift receiver. And by God, these executives will not be outdone by their "friends," even if it means fifty-seven extra hours of overtime for you to figure out how to print out the stupid labels.

Before any of that happens, however, the executive has to update the year's list of the newest and hottest schmoozer contestants in town. Sorry, did I say the executive would be doing this? I meant to say that the executive will hand this daunting task to one of his or her assistants who will immediately pawn it right off on the nearest office production assistant.

As the lucky PA, you must first figure out if every single one of the addresses is correct. We're talking hundreds, maybe thousands, of famous people who make a point of being impossible to reach. Every single year it seems like production assistants all around the county have to come up with ingenious new ways of stalking these illustrious people. The PA can't ask for help from anyone in the office, for this would make the executive wonder why he or she is having the studio pay so much for a person who can't get the job done right.

When you get to your whit's end trying to find these famous celebs—the point when all but five strands of hair have fallen off your head—this is when the producer will say, "Oh, why didn't you just ask me? Bob lives right next door to me."

WARNING: It is important to resist the obvious two questions that follow this stupid comment. The first one being: "You ass, why didn't you tell me that five days ago when you looked the list over and laughed, 'Ha, ha. Good luck trying to find these people!'?"

The second apparent inquiry would be: "If you guys are neighbors, why the hell won't you take the damn present home to him yourself?"

The answer to question number two, besides "You're fired," would be that the executive could never deliver a present in person. You see, the executive would think that his neighbor would think that the studio thinks he or she wasn't worthy enough to have a staff of gofers.

Once you have finally kicked, punched, and completely beaten the hell out of the office computer and have successfully stopped the program from printing the phone numbers on the address labels, then it is customary for the executive to divvy up his "friends" into categories.

Category #1 is for those people whom the executive needs to suck up to at any cost and for any reason. These people either have some sort of privileged dirt on the executive (example: Heidi Fleiss), or they are the Tom Cruises and Julia Roberts of Hollywood whose butts the executive desperately wants to kiss. [Think Rolex watches and bottles of Dom Perignon.]

Category #2 is usually reserved for old friends who can always pull a favor. These are the people who can generally get an A-list talent attached to a project with a couple of phone calls. Or they are the people who can make sure your boss will always have a job in this business—even if your boss has screwed up a half dozen other films. [Think Lakers tickets and rare vintage wines.]

Category #3 is for those that the boss has to give something to. This is the category devoted to the "token gift" kind of people—the type who the executive would never have inside his or her home. We're talking about boutique agents, writers, B-list actors, and the office's assistants (including the dutiful office production assistants). [Think stale mini cakes from a former film shoot and dumb pens with the company's misspelled logo.]

The presents, bought in bulk for that extra personal touch, then need to be picked up. Sometimes semi-trucks are required. Though, usually a PA's beat up, old two-door vehicle is the more preferred option for the frugal executive scrooges. When the execs realize how much the season of joy is costing them, they usually get even tighter with their pennies than normal.

After you bring back the goods, you will unload them at the office in between trips. This means crates of wine, boxes of cakes and piles of cards—not to be mixed with the endless incoming gifts, of course—will be stacked all over the lobby, under the couches, in the bookshelves, etc.

Basically the office work space should sufficiently diminish by about seventy-five percent. At first everyone will think it's funny. Then two hours later the staff will become irritated with you for creating such a mess. This warm cheer can be expected to last until vacation time.

After all the goods are gathered, guess who has to deliver all this crap?! Depending on how much your boss distrusts the U.S. Postal Service, you should plan on getting to know Los Angeles County pretty darn well within those joyous weeks of December. That means reloading all the junk (now wrapped and properly labeled, thank you) back into your little, abused car. Don't expect anyone to help you with the physical labor, but you must trust that your co-workers are there for you emotionally. They'll just hide it by screaming, "Get this stuff out of my way!"

The first few deliveries to the celebrities' houses are kind of cool. No matter how numb one can become with the industry's self-styled pomp and circumstance, who can resist the chance to meet Sly Stallone or Cher at his or her home? No matter how nonchalant a PA is about the whole celebrity game, it's easy to remember why we initially went into this profession.

You'll ring the doorbell only to find a super-jaded housekeeper who speaks no English—at least that's what she'd like you to believe so she doesn't have to answer stupid questions about her boss. In a mechanical way, as though she's done this before, she'll take the package and throw it onto a tower-sized pile of other gifts from Hollywood fakes. In fact, this poor housekeeper has probably opened the door a hundred and seventy six times that morning alone to find bright-eyed production assistants trying to get a glimpse of her movie star boss. Frankly this housekeeper has better things to do than answer the door. The soap operas are on and her boss is off in some European country visiting his illegitimate children for the holidays.

Vacation, All I Ever Wanted...

Darlene was excited for a vacation. Not hers, her boss Tom's. She was relieved this guy was going far, far away to Aruba.

Darlene had been Tom's PA for nearly a year. That was long enough for her to need a break from his obsessive-compulsive behavior, his constant second-guessing, his nagging, and his need to always know where she was going. Basically he was a pretty decent guy...for a director...but he was still *the boss*.

A couple weeks before the trip, he was busy buying swim shorts while Darlene was creating a stack of magazines that she hadn't had a chance to read in months.

While Tom was confirming the rental car details, Darlene was planning each night she'd finally be getting home at a decent hour.

He was stopping his newspaper delivery for two weeks. She was imagining all the long lunches she would be taking.

He was firing his kids' nanny. She was…trying to figure out why he was firing his kids' nanny.

"Darlene?" he asked, "We need someone to baby-sit the kids in Aruba. Would you like to go?"

She was speechless. She was beside herself. She was ecstatic to be invited on an all-expense paid trip to paradise. She was grossed out at the thought of seeing Tom in his bathing suit. But come on, it was Aruba.

"OKAY!" she blurted a little too loudly.

"Great. We leave in two weeks."

Screw the plans to take it easy. She had clothes to buy, bags to pack, friends to brag to. She was going to party in the sun with a tropical drink in each hand. She was going to hook up with some hot, tan men. She was going to look fabulous in her new bikini that would show off her beautiful, newly liposuctioned hips.

Within three hours of the invitation, Darlene had called everyone she'd met since birth to boast, spent four week's salary on beachwear, and raided all the Bloomingdale's cosmetic counters for the most "natural looking" make-up. She was set and ready to go—with a mere one week, six days, and eight hours to spare. Perfect, she thought. She still had time to get waxed.

Darlene waited with tortured anticipation for her free dream vacation to start. She couldn't wait to party with the natives. She was salivating at the thought of dancing on the beach. She was dying of impatience when *finally* the day of departure arrived.

She met up with Tom and his family at LAX as scheduled. She carefully looked the family over. Funny, she never thought to ask how many kids he had. She knew of two but he never mentioned the other two stepchildren. All in all, the kids ranged in ages from six to thirteen. Gulp!

Following the horrendously long plane trip with the rambunctious kids, she figured she would ditch them all for a few hours before dinner. That was before she realized she would be sharing a hotel room with the two youngest ragamuffins. There was no escape! Her life had turned into a ghastly horror film. She looked at the kids, they looked back at her with fiendish smirks before they pounced on her. "Hey! Watch the silicone!" she yelped.

Darlene spent two entire weeks of waking hours tending to the biggest high energy, spoiled brats on Earth. Normally a great lover of children, Darlene was now ready to kill them all. She even tried to stage "cock fights" between the kids before Tom's wife put a stop to that.

Whenever they went out to the beach, if they ever went outdoors at all, Darlene was usually buried under sand. The kids thought that was good fun. Most of their day, however, was spent in the hotel lobby playing cards. All the children were fair-skinned and their mother was a freak about not letting them sizzle like bacon.

To break up the monotony of their Go Fish games, Darlene would shuffle the cards really hard so they'd go flying across the lobby's slick tile floor. The kids were onto her sneaky tactics, but they'd go and pick up every single card so she'd have to sit there and continue playing. It was basically a symbiotic hatred.

At night, Tom and his wife were out dancing and living it up. Back at the hotel room, the kids were hovered in front of the television watching pay-per-view cartoons. Darlene was ready to throw one of the imps through the TV set. That would've made *Pokemon* a little more bearable.

Darlene was not happy at the idea of coming home without the slightest hint of a tan. She might as well have gone to Alaska in December. To top it all off, while they were in the middle of tropical paradise, one of the little twerps managed to get the flu!

At the end of the two weeks, Darlene couldn't get on the return flight fast enough. The only thing she brought home as a souvenir was the flu and a black eye when the eldest miscreant thought it would be funny to trip her in the dark.

CHAPTER THIRTEEN
A Reality Check

Why do we put ourselves through this torture we call love for a business that eats us up and spits us out? Why do we give sweat, blood, and tears to a town that doesn't even know our names?

Sure it may seem like that now and again, but we all know we belong in this industry. We all want the same thing—a chance to create great art, become famous, and make a hell of a lot of money.

The bottom line is: everyone has to pay his or her dues before becoming the top dog. And remember, if you run with the big horses long enough when you're young, you will eventually become one of them. Thus, later in your career you, too, will be able to poop on the little colts.

Top People with Whom the PA Wants to Hobnob	Top People the PA Will be Stuck with Instead
Big-time actor	Big-time actor's personal assistant
Big-time actor	Big-time actor's personal trainer
Big-time actor	Big-time actor's publicist
Big-time actor	Big-time actor's sibling who's also trying to become an actor by riding on big bro/sis' coattails.

Big-time actor	Big-time actor's stand-in
Big-time actor	Every single extra in L.A.
Big-time actor	Waiters of big-time actor's favorite health food restaurants.
Actor's multi-millionaire agent	Actor's multi-millionaire agent's secretary.
Studio exec	Studio guard
Oscar-winning director	Video store clerk who will rent you Oscar-winning director's film.
Oscar-winning director	Craft service person from whom PA gets Oscar-winning director's snacks.
Producer	Nazi receptionist with a headset simultaneously answering 27,000 calls and sorting 59,000 lbs of mail while writing her own screenplay.
Producer	Producer's young unloved step-child who PA will be stuck trying to amuse.
Producer	Newsstand worker from whom PA will buy the most obscure newspapers generated thousands of miles away.
Producer	The guys and gals of Office Depot, Costco, and the grocery store.
Producer	The friendly folks at FedEx and UPS.
Producer	The water delivery guy.
Producer	The copy machine repairman.
Producer	The producer's pool man.

Top 20 Things a PA Should Not Say While on the Job

"Are you a PA too?" to the director.

"I think I'm going to knock off work early today."

"So what's the budget on this sucker?" to the producer.

"No, **you** do it!" to anyone.

"What!? Where's the rest of my paycheck?"

"What's your name?" to an actor.

"What have you been in?" to a semi-famous actor, especially if he or she is the biggest name in your show.

"How did you become the boss?"

"How much do you make?"

"I'm a little tired. I'm going to lie down in one of those nice, big trailers."

"Who wrote this script? It sucks."

"You call that acting?"

"I'm still waiting for that latte I ordered, folks" while sitting in the director's chair.

"You know, I just don't feel like driving today."

"He/she should use a body double" during a nude scene.

"Yeah, like someone's really going to pay money to watch this."

"I'll get reimbursed for my car expenses, right?"

"I think I'll order out for my lunch and expense it to the company."

"Mellow out, we're only making entertainment here."

"Are those real?"

The End

Printed in the United States
119039LV00001B/349/A